D0045923

THE
RECKONING

Also by Mary L. Trump, Ph.D.

Too Much and Never Enough

THE RECKONING

OUR NATION'S TRAUMA AND FINDING A WAY TO HEAL

MARY L. TRUMP, Ph.D.

ST. MARTIN'S PRESS
NEW YORK

First published in the United States by St. Martin's Press,
an imprint of St. Martin's Publishing Group

THE RECKONING. Copyright © 2021 by Compson Enterprises LLC. All rights reserved.
Printed in the United States of America. For information, address
St. Martin's Publishing Group, 120 Broadway, New York, NY 10271.

www.stmartins.com

The Library of Congress Cataloging-in-Publication Data is available upon request.

ISBN 978-1-250-27845-6 (hardcover)
ISBN 978-1-250-27985-9 (signed edition)
ISBN 978-1-250-28017-6 (international edition, sold outside the U.S.,
subject to rights availability)
ISBN 978-1-250-27846-3 (ebook)

Our books may be purchased in bulk for promotional, educational, or business use.
Please contact your local bookseller or the Macmillan Corporate and Premium Sales
Department at 1-800-221-7945, extension 5442, or by email at
MacmillanSpecialMarkets@macmillan.com.

First Edition: 2021

10 9 8 7 6 5 4 3 2 1

To Avary

Contents

CONTENTS

PART IV: THE RECKONING

THE
RECKONING

Introduction

The insurrection on January 6, 2021, shouldn't have come as a surprise—my uncle Donald had been sowing the seeds of discontent for two months and promoting division and grievance for four years. It was a watershed moment—deliberate, planned, incited, yet another assault aimed squarely at everything I had always thought this country stood for. America is a deeply imperfect country—a country that has never actually been a democracy for all of its people, just for a privileged majority—but it always had the potential to become that hoped-for more perfect union. Did the last four years push us further from that goal, or did they simply bring to light that we were never as close to it as we* thought?

This country was born in trauma—trauma inflicted on the native inhabitants of a land from which they were forcibly removed, trauma

---

* A note on pronouns: When I say "we," I am generally referring to white Americans. I have no sympathy for or allegiance to the role of the white majority in our history, or to the brutality of white supremacy, but it would be disingenuous to pretend that I haven't benefited enormously from a system that has kept whites at the top of the racial hierarchy we invented.

sustained by the generations that have succeeded the kidnapped and enslaved Africans who'd been brought to a continent both foreign and hostile, the trauma of those bystanders who failed to intervene when they could, those who could not intervene at all, and even those who committed the atrocities and continued to perpetuate a system that benefited them at the devastating expense of so many others.

In order to understand our current situation, we have to assess the extent of the impact of those early traumas, as well as the knock-on effects of not only ignoring them but pretending we have somehow transcended them. We most certainly have not; 2020, and the three years before, and the last many decades have borne that out.

When we think of trauma, we typically imagine dramatic, violent, singular events—rape, a car accident, a mortar shell exploding. Trauma can be quiet and slow, too, occurring over time in a tense drama of sameness, of hopelessness, of unbearable isolation and loneliness, of helplessness. We often fail to recognize that we are being traumatized *while* we are being traumatized.

When I started to write this book, in October 2020, I was focused on the historical trends that have combined to leave us vulnerable in the wake of COVID-19, the intersecting economic crisis, and the looming mental health crisis. New York, where I live, had already been on a fairly severe lockdown since March. Our numbers had improved by the fall but, having failed to heed the warning of our experience, COVID cases were spiking throughout the rest of the country.

I wondered what it might be like to emerge into a world altered by months of separation, isolation, and division. How would the long-term effects of inactivity, economic uncertainty, boredom, fear of death, and the stress accumulated from all of those things manifest themselves? What form would the trauma take—of not knowing if you carried a virus that could kill you or those you love, of feeling like you were taking your life in your hands every time you left your home, of not knowing when it would end, of the most simple tasks being complicated by fear, of constant worrying about your children? How would the trauma play out if you were an essential frontline worker—stocking shelves, making deliveries, working in a COVID ICU—who could do very little to avoid the risk of coming into contact with the virus? And to that burden add the betrayal by our government: completely unwilling to help us through this unprecedented-in-our-lifetime horror, and actually allowing the horror to happen, allowing it to worsen.

Things became much more complicated by the November election. COVID time had already wreaked its havoc, but election time was somehow worse. It's one thing not to know when something will end, it's another thing entirely to know that something will end, but you can't see how. To me, the November 3 election loomed like a wall, obsidian and monolithic, obscuring all light and beyond which there was no imagining. Even after Election Day passed, we had an uneasy four days during which the results were still unknown, giving Donald an opportunity to claim a victory he had not won and to continue the project he'd embarked on months earlier: to undermine people's faith in the ultimate outcome if Joe Biden won. After November 7, when it seemed we had finally dodged the bullet this country wouldn't survive, the situation grew more dangerous, not because Donald continued to tell the Big Lie, but because, instead of silencing him by acknowledging the Biden-Harris victory, members of the Republican Party remained silent, offered excuses for the delay in conceding, or, worst of all, repeated the Big Lie and championed Donald's attempts to undermine the incoming administration, which included more than sixty lawsuits, all but one of which he lost or were rejected by the court before trial.

He continued to have rallies in which COVID was spread with the same carelessness as his lies.

He continued to disseminate disinformation on Twitter with the dual purpose of deflecting attention from his decisive loss (while it is true that he received more votes than any Oval Office occupant in history, Joe Biden received at least seven million *more* votes than that) and keeping his base angry, overheated, and feeling cheated.

Too many people wanted to believe Donald. Too many people were susceptible to his ability to appear aggrieved on their behalf. Too many people had wanted him to win. Seventy-four million people, in fact—despite, or because of, the four years of incompetence, cruelty, criminality, grifting, unconstitutional behavior, treachery, treason, and most breathtaking of all, the fact that almost three hundred thousand Americans had died by Election Day as a direct result of Donald's willfully malicious inaction. But for him, we would not have become so divided. But for him, a simple lifesaving maneuver like wearing a mask would not have become politicized. But for him, we would not have suffered a mass casualty event in this country every day, for month after month after month.

When we're all suffering versions of the same trauma simultaneously but separately, what can be shared? Betrayal by the government and by people in our communities destroys our sense of security. To be traumatized is to be initiated into a world without trust. It is to be burdened with all of the darkness the world contains and deprived of its considerable light.

Trauma can be compounded when multiple traumatizing events occur in the same time frame. You would think, for example, that a nurse in a COVID ward would only have to deal with the trauma of being a nurse in a COVID ward. But then her trauma is compounded by the fact that the ostensible leader of the free world is accusing frontline medical workers of stealing personal protective equipment (PPE) and blaming them for the PPE shortage. And then compounded even further by the fact, as at least one nurse reported, that her patients who are dying in front of her eyes from COVID-19 believe COVID is a hoax. And finally, her trauma undermines her entire professional identity when fellow nurses who, despite having witnessed firsthand the devastation COVID can cause to the human body, are hesitant to take the vaccine.

The collective personal trauma of having our country knocked to its knees by the least worthy person I can imagine, and an extraordinarily clear sense that we came very close to losing everything—our democracy most importantly—made me realize that this book couldn't simply address the trauma caused by the intersecting crises caused by COVID; it also had to address the trauma caused by the political crisis that exposed the long-standing fragility of our democracy.

I have heard people say, "This is not who we are," but right now this is precisely who we are. Thanks to an outdated and inherently biased political structure, exemplified by the undemocratic electoral college, which has repeatedly put the losing Republican candidate in office, and a divided Senate in which one "half" of the membership represents forty-one million fewer citizens than the other, we are a nation in which a virulent minority has an outsized voice and the majority—underrepresented and forced into a bystander role—suffers mightily in silence. We are going to be dealing with the consequences of the Trump administration, the pandemic, and particularly the insurrection of January 6, for a very, very long time, just as we are going to be confronting the fact that seventy-four million people wanted four more years of whatever they thought they got in the last four.

It may have taken somebody like Donald to hold up the mirror in which we finally are able to see ourselves, but the possibility of somebody like him finding his way to the Oval Office was decades in the making. He is the symptom of a disease that has existed in the body politic from this country's inception, which has, because of our failures to root it out, let alone acknowledge it, metastasized, infecting his followers and affecting the rest of us in ways we may not completely understand for the foreseeable future. From increasing levels of rage and hatred on the one side to increasing levels of helplessness, stress, and despair on the other, we are heading toward an even darker period in our nation's history.

If we look at our experiences as individuals—our isolation, our fears—and extrapolate outward to our experiences as a society—our dissolution, our daily incidents of violence, our loss of power and agency on the world stage—we can begin to understand that the cascade of largely avoidable depredations on our sovereignty, our humanity, and our sense of justice has, over time, left us not just unprepared for one of the worst periods in our history but uniquely vulnerable both emotionally and psychologically.

I come to this not only as somebody who understands from a clinical perspective the havoc unresolved trauma can wreak on a psyche, but as somebody diagnosed with Complex Post-Traumatic Stress Disorder. On the gloomy morning following Election Night 2016, I wrote down the following: "demeaned, diminished, debased." For months I alternated among states of dissociation, rage, and befuddlement. Once or twice a day, the reality that the so-called leader of the free world was my uncle hit me with the force of a punch to the solar plexus. I kept thinking about those three words I'd written and how America would be forever tainted by what it had done.

By the time I reluctantly accepted an invitation to an April 2017

birthday party at the White House for my aunts Maryanne and Elizabeth, I was in the worst psychological shape of my life.

Several months later, I made the decision to leave my home in New
York and go to a treatment center in Tucson that specializes in PTSD,
among other things. I would be there for weeks, excavating decades-old
wounds and trying to figure out why my uncle Donald's elevation to the
White House had so undone me.

Nobody used last names at the residential program since many of my
fellow patients were there for substance addictions. Even so, I found it
unthinkable that anyone should find out who I was or, more relevantly,
who my uncle was. Long before my uncle had entered the political realm,
I had never admitted to anyone that I belonged to the Trump family. The
very first time somebody asked, "Are you related?" I was paying for a
plane ticket. "No," I said. The man behind the counter said in all seriousness, "Obviously. If you were, you'd have your own plane." This
assumption was so far beyond the reality of my life that when the inevitable question came any time I used a credit card, I continued to say, "No."
The response was usually some variation of "I bet you wish you were."

The first few days I spent in the Arizona desert, I was angry beyond
words, and I carried my rage like a shield. Outside of group and individual therapy, I didn't speak to another human being for the first five
days I was there. Other than calling my daughter to check in every day,
I had no interest in what was going on in the wider world. There was no
one else I needed to speak to, no news I needed to hear.

So in the desert, I attempted to chart the territory of my trauma. I
was a shoddy cartographer, and often lost my way, forced to detour
by my desperate need to avoid the very thing that would help me get
home—but facing the trauma was the only way to deal with it, so during
those weeks in the desert, that's what I did.

As my stay came to a close, I booked a 5:00 A.M. flight, and stayed at a hotel near the airport the night before I left. When I arrived in the lobby at 3:30 A.M. to catch the airport shuttle, I noticed a bank of five televisions set high up on the wall, each set to a different channel. Donald was on every single one.

As Donald was for me, he was for this country: what therapists call a "presenting problem." He may have triggered my PTSD, but my original trauma resulted from something that had happened to me a very long time ago, when I was very young and just at the beginning of my life. Post-traumatic wounds don't disappear, although they can be buried. But no matter how deep down they've been submerged, they inevitably surface, taking us by surprise and forcing us either to confront them at long last or to get out our shovels to dig them under again.

What does the fallout from the calamitous year that was 2020 have to do with this country's origin story? I would argue, everything. In this book, I'm going to talk about the trail of impunity, silence, and complicity that winds its way through every generation of our history, from the economic, social, and moral justifications for slavery and Native American genocide, through the failures of Reconstruction, the horrific legal, quasi-legal, and extralegal quagmire in which Jim Crow expanded alongside the cultural expectations and disappearing of oral history that followed both world wars and the 1918 pandemic. The story of our nation is shot through with contradictions that have never been reconciled, hypocrisies that have been brazened through, and crimes against humanity that have been folded into our story of democracy.

These things are all connected—our tragic beginnings; the ensuing transgenerational trauma inflicted on both the overwhelmed Native

American and enslaved African populations; the white majority's tendency to exclude perceived out-groups from the protection of civil society; the evolution and reemergence of white supremacy; our society's insistence upon silencing those who have suffered because of our cruelty, indifference, and ineptitude; the economic and racial disparities that have only worsened since 2016; our devaluing of human life; the increase in anti-Black policies like voter suppression and gerrymandering; the resurgence of lynching as a means of terror and control. We are a nation shackled by a cultural imperative to move on from the pain of war, mass death, disease, and government-sanctioned barbarity in the name of "peace" or "healing" or "a return to normal," when all we've really been doing is preserving the unchecked impunity of the powerful to inflict pain again and again and again.

Our current trauma is the culmination of our history, the logical outcome of the stories we tell ourselves, the myths we embrace, and the lies we perpetuate. Trauma shapes us in ways we may not be aware of, and will always do so unless we face what has happened to us, what we've done to ourselves, what we've done to each other. Without looking through that lens, we cannot fully understand what has unfolded. My goal is not only to define trauma as it relates to us today but also to try to understand how trauma lives on from one generation to the next so we can find a better way forward. Our country is on fire—literally, metaphorically—ravaged by flames, disease, and civic strife, all of which have been fanned by the willful indifference of a significant minority. The danger has abated but not passed. The flames are waiting to jump the line.

PART I

A Short History of American Failure: 1865—2020

CHAPTER 1

Atrocities

Technically, a "lynching" doesn't require that the victim be hanged, even though hanging is what people usually think of when they hear the word. Rather, it refers to any extralegal mob action against an individual or individuals. In fact, hanging is the least of what happened to the more than sixty-five hundred Black men, women, and children who are known to have been murdered at the hands of white mobs from 1865 to 1950. The actual number of people killed was almost certainly much higher, and the vast majority of the victims had committed no crime, broken no social convention.

That is likely true of Luther Holbert, who was accused of killing a wealthy plantation owner named James Eastland during a dispute, and certainly true of his wife, who was accused of nothing and was not named in news reports. The two were hunted by a white mob through a hundred miles of swamps and brambles before being cornered by hunting dogs. Killing the Holberts at the place they were caught would not have served the cause of "justice." Instead, they were brought back to the woods near Doddsville, Mississippi, the town from which they'd been driven, and tied to a tree. While a pyre was prepared, the men nearest them amputated Mr. and Mrs. Holbert's fingers one by one and handed the severed digits out to the crowd of bystanders, which had grown to over six hundred men, women, and children, as souvenirs. Then the couple's ears were cut off and also distributed. Luther Holbert was beaten so severely that one of his eyes popped out of its socket, hanging "by a shred." Even that wasn't enough. Large corkscrews were produced and inserted into and pulled out from the Holberts' legs, torsos, and arms, over and over, until there was no more sport in it. Only then was the fire set. They were still alive.

This wasn't an isolated act of barbarity. And it didn't happen in the antebellum South. Mr. and Mrs. Holbert were free American citizens who were tortured and murdered in 1904, four decades after the end of the Civil War and just a year before one of my grandfathers was born. Apart from the couple, nobody who participated was held accountable.

The failures of Reconstruction, the period that immediately followed the Civil War, are legion, but our country's profound issues around race reach much further back, to a time when the idea of race, and by extension racial division, was constructed in order to justify the enslavement and subjugation of Blacks. The postwar climate of leniency toward the treasonous leaders of the Confederacy, the lack of vigilance in protecting freed Black men and women, and the backsliding toward the ethos of the prewar South aren't at all surprising, but the implications of these things continue to affect all of us to this day, and help to explain not only why we continue to be so divided but why we hate each other so much.

Reconstruction started with great promise. The Union had been saved and more than four million people were granted their freedom via the Thirteenth Amendment, which was ratified in December 1865. Although the question of slavery in the South had been resolved, Southern society would need to rebuild without the institution that had been the foundation of its economy and culture for centuries. The questions of how North and South would resolve their still-intense differences and how the newly freed men and women would be integrated into a society that had exploited and excluded them for almost 250 years remained to be answered.

Although now free, millions of Blacks emerged from their bondage destitute and without any appreciable means of support. Lincoln's Proclamation of Amnesty and Reconstruction, issued eleven months after the 1863 Emancipation Proclamation, contained language that did not bode well for the promise of an integrated democracy. Although it required Southern states to abolish slavery, they were permitted to deal with Blacks in a way "consistent . . . with their present condition as a laboring, landless, and homeless class." This paternalistic and degrading language implied not only that the enslaved were better off in the care of their "masters" and destined to be laborers (in this context, plantation workers), but more troublingly it suggested that the U.S. government viewed freedmen and freedwomen as having no rights to the wealth they had produced, which had enriched North and South alike.

Many Republicans, at the time the pro-abolition party, believed that the only way to ensure a smooth transition from slavery to freedom, and ensure freedmen and freedwomen's rightful place in society as citizens, was targeted and sustained assistance. Toward this end, the Freedmen's Bureau was established in March 1865. Its mandate included providing food, fuel, and other kinds of aid, establishing schools, moderating disputes between whites and Blacks, introducing a system of free labor, and ensuring equal justice. General William Tecumseh Sherman, in a letter to the Bureau's commissioner, General Oliver Howard, wrote, "I fear you have Hercules' task." Giving Southern Blacks access to land was also seen as an essential part of its mandate. George Julian, a white congressman from Indiana and a fierce advocate of abolition, insisted that without land reform, speculators would reduce freedmen (as well as poor whites) to a situation "more galling than slavery itself."

Early in 1865, General Sherman was encouraged by Secretary of War Edwin Stanton to meet with twenty leaders of the Savannah, Georgia, Black community. When Garrison Frazer, one of those leaders, was asked at the meeting to define freedom and describe the manner in which he believed freedmen and freedwomen could sustain themselves, he said, "The freedom . . . is taking us from under the yoke of bondage, and placing us where we could reap the fruit of our own labor, take care of ourselves and assist the Government in maintaining our freedom. The way we can best take care of ourselves is to have land, and turn it and till it by our own labor—that is, by the labor of the women and children and old men."

Four days after this meeting, Sherman issued Special Field Order 15 and ordered that four hundred thousand acres of coastline from Charleston, South Carolina, south to Florida near Jacksonville be confiscated and divided into forty-acre plots. Brigadier General Rufus Saxton, the Bureau chief for South Carolina, Georgia, and Florida, settled thousands of Black people on these lands, and the Bureau commissioner, General Howard, followed suit, issuing an order of his own in July that as many freedmen and freedwomen be settled on these lands as quickly as possible.

But the assassination of Abraham Lincoln on April 14, 1865, a mere four days after General Robert E. Lee, commander of the Confederate army, surrendered to the Union army, threw the fate of Reconstruction into serious doubt before it had even begun. Radical Republicans—anti-slavery and pro-suffrage—were in control of Congress, but Democrat Andrew Johnson, Lincoln's successor, was a former enslaver whose sympathies lay with the conquered South.

Despite the hardships of destitution, dislocations, and hostility, Blacks in the South began the complex and difficult work of building communities and making strides in three major areas—education, religion, and politics. As much as 80 percent of the Black population was illiterate at war's end because Black literacy had been considered a threat to white dominance by the planter class. Before the Civil War, learning how to read and write was almost universally prohibited by enslavers, and any attempts to do so were severely punished. Even plantation owners who sought to teach the enslaved were heavily fined. This hostility also enforced the condition of dependence. As John W. Fields, who had been enslaved since birth, said, "Our ignorance was the greatest hold the South had on us."

General Howard shared Southern Blacks' views on the importance of education for advancing their interests, and overseeing schools was an important mission for the overstretched agency. Congress, however, had been ambivalent about the necessity of the Bureau in the first place and conflicted about its mission, so although the Bureau could oversee schools, it was not provided with the funds necessary to establish them.

Before the war, there had barely been a system of public education in the South. The children of rich whites went to private schools and the rest had to fend for themselves. The push among freed Blacks for state-funded education benefited all children, and by the end of Reconstruction over six hundred thousand Black children were attending Black schools. Similarly, the membership of Black Baptist churches swelled to 1.3 million by the 1880s.

Freedmen and freedwomen knew, however, that the single most important task for sustaining and extending their gains as citizens was to secure suffrage for all Black males. With the ratification of the Fifteenth Amendment in 1870, the franchise was extended and a dynamic political culture was formed in Black communities. Very quickly, strides were made to get Black men elected at all levels of government, and as many as two thousand succeeded.

In 1870, Hiram Revels was chosen by the Mississippi state legislature to fill the Senate seat vacated by Albert Brown when the state seceded from the Union. Revels was confirmed in the Senate by a vote of 48–8 to serve the remaining year of the term. Upon his confirmation, Massachusetts senator Charles Sumner said, "All men are created equal, says the great Declaration, and now a great act attests this verity. Today we make the Declaration a reality. . . . The Declaration was only half established by Independence. The greatest duty remained behind. In assuring the equal rights of all we complete the work."

Four years later, Blanche Bruce, also from Mississippi, was elected and became in 1875 the first Black American senator to serve a full term. Although the momentousness of these achievements cannot be denied, neither can the fact that it would be another ninety-two years before another Black American served in the United States Senate, which shows just how fleeting the promise of Reconstruction really was. (To date, there have still been only eleven Black senators total in the more than 150 years since Hiram Revels's election.)

One early problem in the transition from war to Reconstruction was that Lincoln never put a plan in place. He was interested in maintaining party unity and public support, particularly on the issue of Black suffrage, but he was also concerned that he not be seen as dictating to the South. Without swift and decisive action, questions that had been plaguing the country since its inception remained unsettled and carried the risk of hardening attitudes on both sides. Many people despaired that the question—namely, "What shall we do with the Negro?"—could be resolved at all.

And then there was the problem of the president who presided over the first years of Reconstruction. Before the war, Andrew Johnson had enslaved nine people, and before the 1863 Emancipation Proclamation went into effect he persuaded Lincoln to exempt Tennessee, his home state, from the provision to free its enslaved people.

Less than a month after taking office, Johnson began issuing pardons to white Southerners who "directly or indirectly participated in the existing rebellion." Blacks were not invited to participate in the drafting of new Southern state constitutions. Instead of requiring the former Confederacy to grant even limited voting rights to Blacks, as Lincoln had been inclined to do, Johnson left the issue up to individual states. The move prompted Representative Thaddeus Stevens to say, "If we leave free Black people to the legislation of their late masters, we had better left them in bondage." By 1866 the number of pardons Johnson had issued had increased to seven thousand.

Worse, he overturned the orders issued by General Sherman and the Freedmen's Bureau that had distributed land to freedmen, effectively evicting Black families from land that had been explicitly set aside for them and returning it to the men who had committed treason for the purposes of enslaving the very people they were once again going to displace. Of the nearly five million Black Americans who lived in the South—90 percent of the entire Black population in the United States—in 1870 only thirty thousand, or 1 percent, owned land—a damning indictment of Johnson's reversal.

It was in the context of these maneuvers that Congress, still missing representatives from the majority of Southern states, passed the Civil Rights Act of 1866, granting Black Americans full citizenship. Johnson vetoed the bill, saying it discriminated "in favor of the Negro, to whom, after long years of bondage, the avenues to freedom and intelligence have just now been suddenly opened. He must of necessity, from his previous unfortunate condition of servitude, be less informed as to the nature and character of institutions" than even foreigners immigrating to the United States.

Congress overrode the veto with a two-thirds majority in both chambers, but this was a crucial moment, and Johnson's rhetoric mattered. The North may have technically won the war, but the country was still at a crossroads and he had the power to sway opinion. He was making it increasingly clear which side he was on.

In the meantime, the Bureau's ability to fulfill its mission was severely hampered at every turn. Not surprisingly, there was a pressing need for doctors to treat freedmen and freedwomen. A medical division was created under the auspices of the Bureau and forty hospitals were set up across the South, but only 120 doctors were assigned to staff them. After requests for additional equipment and personnel were ignored, all forty were closed.

From the beginning, the seemingly insurmountable obstacles to Reconstruction included a failure to anticipate the enormity of the project of healing the rift between North and South, and integrating freedmen and freedwomen into a society that had so recently held them as chattel. Many, perhaps most, Northerners were not terribly concerned about the fate of Blacks beyond emancipation. As one Northern Republican put it, "[I have a] precious poor opinion of niggers . . . a still poorer one of slavery." This attitude was not uncommon, which increasingly became evident as Reconstruction wore on. In a prescient statement, Charles Reason, a Black American educator, said, "The prejudice now felt against [freedmen] for bearing on their own persons the brand of slaves cannot die out immediately."

Failure to gauge not only the scope of the social and economic task at hand but also how deeply entrenched such attitudes had been in the psyches of white people for generations explains why they prevailed. As historian Eric Foner notes, much policy at the time reflected this ambivalence and was also exemplified by the framing of two problems facing the Bureau by an army officer in July 1865: "Two evils against which the Bureau had to contend were cruelty on the part of the employer and shirking on the part of the Negroes."

In the end, "shirking on the part of the Negro" was deemed to be the greater evil, an ugly stereotype of the "lazy Black" that failed to take into account that such "shirking," if it even existed, was likely related to freed people's resentment at being forced to work for their former captors. Yet the Bureau seemed to consider Black reluctance to labor the greater threat to its economic mission. To the very end of Reconstruction, Blacks would insist that those who freed them should protect that freedom.

Another major concern of white legislators was that assistance to Blacks would lead to dependence. As Sea Island teacher William C. Gannett put it, "Thrown upon themselves the speedier will be their salvation." In keeping with a pseudoscientific trope that had been peddled for decades—that Blacks had weak lungs and needed to be forced to perform hard labor in order to strengthen them—work was deemed better medicine than medical care.

After the war, many white elected leaders on both sides worked to diminish Black political power. In his 1867 State of the Union address, President Andrew Johnson said:

If anything can be proved by known facts, if all reasoning upon evidence is not abandoned, it must be acknowledged that in the progress of nations Negroes have shown less capacity for government than any other race of people. No independent government of any form has ever been successful in their hands. On the contrary, wherever they have been left to their own devices they have shown a constant tendency to relapse into barbarism. In the Southern States, however, Congress has undertaken to confer upon them the privilege of the ballot. Just released from slavery, it may be doubted whether as a class they know more than their ancestors how to organize and regulate civil society.

Johnson came down squarely on the anti-suffrage side of the argument time and again. His comments in the 1868 State of the Union are even worse:

The attempt to place the white population under the domination of persons of color in the South has impaired, if not destroyed, the kindly relations that had previously existed between them: and mutual distrust has engendered a feeling of animosity which leading in some instances to collision and bloodshed, has prevented that cooperation between the two races so essential to the success of industrial enterprise in the Southern States.

This was an egregious misrepresentation of both history and the political moment, but coming from the president who was supposed to be overseeing Reconstruction and protecting the freed status of Black people, it was a terrible blow to the morale of those who favored giving Black men the vote. As Frederick Douglass wrote, "Slavery is not abolished until the black man has the ballot."

Johnson's words also gave a boost to the Union's former enemies, who seemed determined to reestablish the old labor order. Through words and deeds from 1865 on, Andrew Johnson seemed inclined not only to allow but to encourage the reestablishment of the South's planter class and its adherence to white supremacy.

The North's attitudes toward Reconstruction and Southern Blacks constituted a willful misreading of the division between Southern whites and Blacks, and failed to acknowledge the *total* culpability of former enslavers or defenders of slavery. This failure to lay blame squarely where it belonged and instead to pander to the perpetrators of the crimes rather than stand up for the victims was succeeded by the lack of will to compensate freedmen and freedwomen appropriately. It made possible a horrifying reversion to an antebellum system of exploitation of coerced labor and the continuance of white supremacy.

How do you convey the horrors of something like the Middle Passage? Words fail, the imagination fails. No visual or pictorial rendering could possibly get across the inhumane conditions, the suffocating stench, the unbearable sounds of human agony, the limitless darkness, the loss of dignity and hope endured (or not) by the twelve million kidnapped Africans who were forced into the cramped, airless holds of slave ships and chained together for weeks, often months, at a time.

So extreme were the conditions that 16 percent—almost two million—of those who were forced to take the journey died on the way.

Twenty percent of the population of colonial America consisted of enslaved people. New York was the slave capital of the colonies for one hundred and fifty years. Over time the colonial economy, particularly in the South, became more and more dependent on the labor of the enslaved. This dependence created the need for more enslaved laborers, and with it the need to justify not only the barbaric practice but the savagery that was used to maintain it.

Slavery in the colonies started out as a form of indentured servitude, which, as a result of the increasing economic imperative, became a unique institution. As soon as survivors of the Middle Passage arrived in North America, the process of "seasoning" began, and they were stripped of their language, their culture, their religion, anything that tied them to their home and their sense of identity. The enslaved were marked out by their race, their status became permanent and heritable (a child born to an enslaved parent would also be enslaved, and so on through the generations), and they were deemed chattel—property to be traded, used as collateral, or disposed of at the owner's will.

In order to sustain this extreme situation, which was implemented and maintained with the utmost brutality by slavers, plantation owners, and overseers, it needed to be justified.

It was necessary to the project of slavery that whites dehumanize Blacks in any way they could—a process that created extreme levels of cognitive dissonance because those who participated in the slave trade knew that those they enslaved were human beings; their knowledge of this, however, meant that creating rationales for their inhumane behavior was necessary; and at the same time they at least claimed to believe in a democratic government and considered themselves "good Christians."

Their rationales included the religious (the brutish nature of the enslaved Africans made them a danger to themselves and others; the structure of slavery would ennoble them and reward them in the afterlife), the paternalistic (Blacks were lazy, childish, and unintelligent and needed the benevolent supervision of their "masters"), and the pseudoscientific (Blacks' allegedly small skulls denoted limited intellectual capacity, so they needed to be protected, while their allegedly large sex organs meant they were promiscuous, and white women needed to be protected from them). In short, they argued, slavery benefited the enslaved, and their white owners were making sacrifices in order to make the enslaved people's lives better.

The idea that Black people had no need for human attachment excused the practice of separating parents from their children. The belief that they had an abnormally high threshold for pain justified the most gruesome punishments, including whipping and other forms of physical torture. James Sims, the so-called father of gynecology, also espoused this belief and performed surgery—without anesthesia, despite its being widely available—on enslaved women who had been loaned to him by their enslavers. Sims also operated on Black infants who suffered from a condition known as "trismus nascentium," or neonatal tetanus, that was caused by living in unsanitary conditions (which was almost always the case in slave quarters on plantations). The "cure" required separating their as-yet-unfused skull bones with an awl. This, too, was done without anesthesia, and all of these babies died during or shortly after the surgery. But the supply of victims for Sims to experiment on was virtually endless.

That anyone believed the divisions could be healed or a free-labor society and a biracial democracy—or even a country in which the races tolerated each other—could be achieved, seems, in retrospect, breathtakingly naïve. The work that was done toward any of those ends was incomplete and unsustained. The Freedmen's Bureau, perhaps the best hope for creating the conditions in which lasting change could take place, was underfunded and short-lived.

Slavery had lasted for centuries. The Americans alive during Reconstruction had been preceded by generations of Black people who had been enslaved or white people poisoned by the beliefs required to justify slavery.

Slaveholders in the South seceded from the Union and incited a civil war in order to retain their right to own other human beings. When the war was over, they gave up slavery unwillingly. The crime of slavery was never acknowledged. No Truth and Reconciliation Commission was formed to render a verdict or hold the perpetrators accountable. Instead, former enslavers remained free to amass power and rebuild the South in the image of the antebellum plantation, with all the crimes against humanity that had entailed.

No, the project to validate the dehumanization and subjugation of Black men, women, and children had been going on for too long. It reached the height of hypocrisy during Reconstruction, when the overarching belief began to take hold that it was *Black* Americans who were the obstacle to national unity.

The Thirteenth, Fourteenth, and Fifteenth Amendments accomplished the astonishing feat of freeing four million people, making all of them U.S. citizens, and extending the franchise to all freedmen. Taken together, they opened the possibility of turning the United States into a truly biracial democracy. But because of the way the amendments were written, in conjunction with increasing indifference and hostility in the North, a desperate opportunism in the South, and a president determined to harm Blacks' chances at every turn, the road was paved for future abuses and backsliding.

In none of these amendments was there language forbidding limits on voting rights, like poll taxes or literacy requirements. The Thirteenth Amendment said nothing specifically about racial equality. The Fifteenth Amendment, which gave freedmen the vote, did not specifically grant Black people the right to hold office because including such a provision would have endangered the support of certain whites in Congress.

It was a phrase in the Thirteenth Amendment, however, that would prove the most damaging to the prospect of Black sovereignty in the South and in a very short period of time erase all of the freedmen's electoral and legislative gains. While it is true that with the ratification of this amendment four million people were freed from bondage, the text of

Section 1 reads, "Neither slavery nor involuntary servitude, except as a punishment for crime whereof the party shall have been duly convicted, shall exist within the United States, or any place subject to their jurisdiction." The clause "except as punishment for a crime whereof the party shall have been duly convicted" would be a fatal blow to the prospect of racial equality and democracy.

The door was left wide open for the implementation of new laws in the South, known as the Black Codes, that would ultimately serve the purpose of regaining control over Black labor. Although the Codes granted some rights to freedmen and freedwomen—the right to testify in court (against other Blacks), to marry, and to own property—they eventually reversed many of the gains made during Reconstruction and paved the way for ever more stringent and punitive restrictions on the freed people's ability to vote, work independently, amass wealth, and, in the end, live freely.

The rationale presented for the necessity of coercive control of Black men, in particular, was their supposed sexual aggressiveness and the danger it posed to white women, which white Southerners believed would lead to "rampant race-mixing and a collapse of civilization." The apocalyptic language underscored both the absurdity and danger of these charges.

The real reason for the Codes was economic, of course. Unable or unwilling to come up with a new system of labor, Southern planters remained convinced that their businesses' financial viability depended on coerced labor. Despite having been treated with astonishing leniency and never having been sufficiently sanctioned for instigating and then losing the Civil War, Southerners felt entitled to reclaim what they believed to be rightly theirs—the four million human beings who represented a monetary value upward of four billion dollars that had been wiped out when the Confederacy surrendered.

The loophole within the Thirteenth Amendment led to the expansion of convict leasing in the South, a system by which prisoners were leased by the state to turpentine farms or plantations for a fee. The convicts were not paid at all, and control of their credit and property was assigned by law to the planters. In order to expand the practice, which proved lucrative (in some states fees from convict leasing were as much as 10 percent of the state's revenue), laws were invented to expand the labor pool. "Vagrancy" and "loitering" were criminalized and carried considerable fines and sentences of up to a year of hard labor. The laws were both discriminatory and vague—vagrancy could mean anything from spending your money the wrong way to being idle, and the "intent to steal" was made a crime in North Carolina—and therefore easy to enforce, and the vast majority of prisoners were Black. As historian Leon F. Litwack writes, "The laws discriminated against them, the courts upheld a double standard of justice, and the police acted as the enforcers." Every person involved in the accusation, the arrest, the indictment, the conviction, and the sentencing, and everyone who enforced the contracts, was white. And many of them still wore their Confederate uniforms.

Leased convicts and debtors were forced to work in conditions that in some cases were worse than those on the plantations where they had previously been enslaved. Working in the sugarcane fields was so dangerous that most laborers died after seven years. The turpentine camps were described by one prison inspector as "a human slaughter pen."

The system of sharecropping, which had sprung up in the place of granting freedmen homesteads, came to resemble a form of indentured servitude itself. Initially, sharecroppers were meant to be seen as partners in or renters of the land they worked, but after a number of court decisions, the sharecropper came to be seen as a wage laborer who remained at the mercy of the planters' accounting of wages at the end of the harvest, which we know was rarely honest. In fact, the sharecropper's debt to the planter seemed only to increase, and he or she was almost never able to get out from under it.

While state governments in the South expanded the circumstances under which Blacks could be subject to convict leasing and peonage, Blacks' options to find other avenues of employment dwindled. Blacks were forbidden from leasing land. In South Carolina, if a Black worker wished to work in a profession other than agriculture or domestic service, an exorbitant annual tax was required. Without any realistic means of support, most Blacks were forced to sign yearly contracts with employers.

Lumbermen and sawmill and turpentine camp operators believed they should be "permitted to control their labor as they saw fit, without any interference from the federal authorities," said U.S. attorney Alexander Akerman, their argument being that without forced labor (basically enslaving people), they wouldn't be able to turn a profit.

While coercion of Black labor was on the rise, the violence against Southern Blacks also escalated at alarming rates, increasing in both intensity and viciousness.

As the Reconstruction years wore on, the Freedmen's Bureau was in effect the only entity that stood between Southern Blacks and the violence being inflicted on them by Southern whites. But there was little the Bureau could do to protect Black communities from white violence, and the Bureau's urgent requests for federal troops were ignored.

Whites claimed they were acting preemptively against Black criminality, which they said would run rampant now that Blacks were free. The paradigm shifted not so subtly from "Blacks as property" to "Blacks as criminals." The real goal of the violence, of course, was to destroy the Republican Party in the South and to disrupt, impede, and finally end the ability of Blacks to exercise their rights as citizens, to maintain independence, or to participate in government at any level.

Despite the steady stream of assaults, injustices, lynchings, mass murders, and terror campaigns against Black individuals, Black families, and Black communities, some prominent Democrats claimed there was no sustained pattern of racially motivated violence aimed at the subjugation of Blacks, while others did nothing to contradict this lie. But almost all of these actions were coordinated by Redeemers (as Democrats in the South were known), former Confederates, enslavers, businessmen, and planters whose goal it was to return the South to its antebellum glory.

The number of Black men, women, and children lost during this period to mass murder, terror attacks, and lynchings is incalculable. As Litwack writes, no "statistical breakdown [could] reveal the barbarity and depravity that so frequently characterized the assaults made on freedmen in the [purported] name of restraining their savagery and depravity." The words "savagery" and "depravity" begin to lose meaning, especially when you consider those words were deployed by whites with the express purpose of demonstrating the savagery and depravity of *Black people*. The extreme violence served two purposes—to terrify freedmen into compliance and to justify the terrorism. The false rationale held that nobody would ever treat another human being the way white Southerners treated Black men, women, and children—therefore, they couldn't possibly be human. The alternative, that the perpetrators of the violence were as vicious and irredeemable as they claimed their victims to be, was unthinkable.

Charles Sumner, the Republican senator from Massachusetts, believed that the Freedmen's Bureau should be permanent and its commissioner a cabinet-level position. Other Republican senators, however, continued to fear that the freedmen and freedwomen would become dependent on Northern help. Despite the massive breadth of the Bureau's portfolio, it was underfunded, understaffed, and from the outset meant to be temporary. An agency tasked with undoing over 250 years of deeply embedded racial hostility, and reforming a culture completely dependent on free labor and white supremacy, was doomed by lack of political will.

By 1873 the end of Reconstruction was practically guaranteed when the postwar economic expansion ended abruptly, thanks in part to over-leveraged financial practices—particularly in the railroad industry—and inflation.

The New York Herald, referring to white Southerners as "our brothers and sisters," claimed they were once again "our fellow citizens." In another New York publication, Blacks were blamed for not making the most of their opportunity to become full participants in American democracy.

After a contentious election in 1876, a bipartisan electoral commission voted to give the presidency to Rutherford B. Hayes. In order to seal the deal, Hayes agreed to withdraw all federal troops from the South. Reconstruction was effectively over. Although some of its accomplishments would be enduring (if stalled), its failures kept in place a powerful and still-wealthy planter class that espoused white supremacist ideals and was determined to fully return to an economic system that depended on coerced and uncompensated labor.

None of the reversals, as Eric Foner has made clear, "would have proved decisive without the campaign of violence that turned the electoral tide in many parts of the South and the weakening of Northern resolve."

Bryan Stevenson, the founder and executive director of the Equal Justice Initiative, said in a *Vox* interview with Ezra Klein in May 2017, "I actually think the great evil of American slavery wasn't involuntary servitude and forced labor. The true evil of American slavery was the narrative we created to justify it. They made up this ideology of white supremacy that cannot be reconciled with our Constitution, that cannot be reconciled with a commitment to fair and just treatment of all people. They made it up so they could feel comfortable."

What freedmen and freedwomen accomplished between 1865 and 1877 was nothing short of astonishing, especially considering the extent and seriousness of the impediments put in their way, from uninterrupted racism and white supremacy to inadequate assistance from the North and campaigns of terrorist violence. Given the climate, it shouldn't be surprising that the gains made at the beginning of Reconstruction, as impressive as they were, proved to be fleeting.

The North won the armed conflict after an extraordinary loss of blood and treasure, but it was at the point of surrender that the South, symbolically and rhetorically, won the war itself.

Two separate events—one in 1896 and the other in 1898—demonstrated how completely Reconstruction had failed. The 1896 Supreme Court decision in *Plessy v. Ferguson,* which upheld the constitutionality of segregation as long as segregated facilities were "equal," proved crushing for the prospects of Black Americans. Two years later, the unveiling of an eighty-eight-foot-tall Confederate monument in Montgomery, Alabama, was a blunt reminder of the enduring belief in white supremacy. Adding insult to injury was the fact that the man who had laid the cornerstone was former Confederate president Jefferson Davis, who, after serving two years in prison, had been released on bond and later pardoned by Andrew Johnson, and would live out his long life unmolested.

The Lost Cause—a myth that had sprung up after the Civil War and was built around a revisionist history that claimed the cause of the war was a heroic dispute over states' rights having nothing to do with slavery and that Southern culture was genteel and honorable—began to gain greater currency as white Southerners continued to consolidate power.

Before Reconstruction was over, Blacks had been effectively disenfranchised by violence and threats of violence. By 1908, ten Southern states had rewritten their constitutions, implementing poll taxes, literacy tests, and other impediments to voting that overwhelmingly disadvantaged Blacks. Completely shut out of participatory government, Blacks were also shut out of job opportunities.

In the Jim Crow South, sharecropping, peonage (binding laborers to indentured servitude as a result of debt), and convict leasing, often described as "slavery by another name" or "worse than slavery," became even more deeply entrenched and ingrained in the economic system. Sharecroppers were given little choice but to buy their supplies, which were marked up from 100 percent to as much as 1,000 percent, on credit at company stores. The cycle of debt thus incurred persisted for generations.

As Blacks were forced into labor situations that increasingly curtailed their freedoms—to support themselves, to move independently—the class structure that pitted no-wage Blacks and low-wage whites against each other came more and more to resemble the situation that had existed in pre–Civil War days.

The violence with which these draconian labor practices were inextricably intertwined did not abate, and both were exacerbated by the unremitting drive of the government and the judiciary to curtail or erase the rights of Black people and sanction extralegal and blatantly illegal acts committed by whites. The Ku Klux Klan, formed in Tennessee on December 24, 1865, was instrumental in this effort. As during Reconstruction, violence against Blacks was neither random nor isolated but rather sustained domestic terrorism aimed at advancing the goals of white supremacy and Black subjugation.

Over the course of the Jim Crow era, from 1877 to 1965, thousands and thousands of lynchings were recorded, and likely many more went unrecorded. Law enforcement not only sanctioned these crimes against humanity, but in many cases participated. The depravity of these lynchings was medieval, a signifier not just of white male superiority but of complete domination. It was the ultimate act of dehumanization of both the victims and the perpetrators.

The people engaged in these acts of depravity were themselves depraved. What appalls is how the depravity was normalized. In photographs of lynchings, the orchestrators, who typically appear proud and self-satisfied, are surrounded by dozens, sometimes hundreds, sometimes thousands, of spectators. As they watched the torture and mutilation, they sipped lemonade and passed around baked goods. Afterward, the onlookers mingled around the still-smoldering corpses, posing for group photos with their children, smiling, relaxed as at a picnic. It reminds me of the children of Nazi concentration camp commanders who laughed at the weak, starving Jews when they passed by, not knowing any better. But 90 percent of the lynchings in this country occurred years and decades before those concentration camps even existed.

Everything continued to be stacked against Black Americans' full entry into American society—propelled by centuries of race-based discrimination and the white supremacy that created it. The oppression was deliberate, sustained, and multidimensional. Segregation was not a matter of preference, then or now. The average American had no idea just how carefully engineered segregation—of schools, of jobs, and of housing—actually was. At the local, state, and federal levels, laws were enacted and a wide array of government agencies (the Federal Housing Authority, the United States Housing Authority, the Public Works Administration) were deployed to ensure that Black Americans lived separately from and in conditions inferior to those of white Americans.

Segregation was structured and enforced by increasingly Byzantine legal and performative measures that were expensive, disruptive, humiliating to Blacks, and bizarre in their extremity. And although the stereotypical expressions of segregation (separate water fountains and train cars) were confined to the South, housing and school segregation existed across the country.

To this day, most white Americans think that geographic segregation was self-selecting, that Blacks chose to live separately from whites. The truth, as usual, is more sinister, and it led to another massive theft of resources that made it difficult if not impossible for Blacks to enter the ranks of the middle class. Redlining, the discriminatory practice of denying services like mortgages or business loans, was rampant across the country throughout the Jim Crow era. White people were allowed to buy houses with low-interest mortgages and receive free college educations. In the first instance this enabled them to amass wealth and equity, in the second it enabled them to live free of often crushing debt. Blacks were denied these opportunities, robbing them of untold wealth, the result of which has reverberated through succeeding generations.

As Richard Rothstein points out in *The Color of Law,* "Residential racial segregation by state action is a violation of our Constitution and its Bill of Rights. The Fifth Amendment, written by our Founding Fathers, prohibits the federal government from treating citizens unfairly. The Thirteenth Amendment, adopted immediately after the Civil War, prohibits slavery or, in general, treating Black Americans as second-class citizens, while the Fourteenth Amendment, also adopted after the Civil War, prohibits states, or their local governments, from treating people either unfairly or unequally." Just because segregation has been repeatedly upheld by the Supreme Court doesn't mean it's constitutional; it simply means the court came to erroneous conclusions and wrote bad decisions based on them. After all, the first Civil Rights Act has been prohibiting housing segregation since 1866.

School segregation inevitably followed housing segregation. In 1954 the Supreme Court sought to remedy this problem, declaring in its *Brown v. Board of Education of Topeka* decision that "separate educational facilities are inherently unequal." The reactions were swift, and opposition across the South was organized and violent.

Democrats in Congress drafted the Southern Manifesto:

This unwarranted exercise of power by the Court, contrary to the Constitution, is creating chaos and confusion in the States principally affected. It is destroying the amicable relations between the white and Negro races that have been created through 90 years of patient effort by the good people of both races. It has planted hatred and suspicion where there has been heretofore friendship and understanding.

The decision was appealed, and a year later the court delegated desegregation to the district courts, where it was to be carried out "with all deliberate speed," a meaningless phrase that left the matter open-ended and the ruling unenforceable.

Brown had unintended consequences that made the initial decision seem a hollow victory. Ripping children out of their schools in the name of integration had devastating repercussions for Black schools and the communities they served. As the psychologist Milton Schwebel put it, "What many of us fighting for social justice didn't anticipate was the dark cloud that would hover over us for so very long. The loss of jobs for African-American teachers and administrators, the black students who would have to leave their schools and enter new schools with fear and trepidation, the black parents who once had a voice in their local schools but would now be silenced in the desegregated schools because integration was mostly one way. Black schools closed."

From the moment the Civil War ended, this country made a choice to undermine and reverse the very cause for which that war was fought. It took only twelve years for Reconstruction to run its course, as if in that short span of time a still deeply divided country could undo and emerge united from over two and a half centuries of prejudices and the culture, institutions, and lies that perpetuated them. At every turn, white men, even Southern traitors, were given the benefit of the doubt, while Blacks were derided for their supposed inferiority and lack of skills or blamed for their circumstances. The commitment to racial hierarchy was too deeply entrenched and, for many whites, psychologically necessary. As the Equal Justice Initiative points out, "'Freeing' the nation's masses of enslaved Black people without undertaking the work to deconstruct the false narrative of white supremacy doomed those freed people and generations of their descendants to a fate of second-class citizenship," or worse.

While narrowly focused on segregation in public schools, *Brown v. Board of Education* did not really overturn *Plessy v. Ferguson*, the 1896 case that first challenged segregation of public facilities (in that particular case, a train in Louisiana). In that ruling, Justice Henry Billings Brown wrote that it was not up to the Constitution to "abolish distinctions based upon color" or put the two races "upon the same plane." So with the exception of education, "separate but equal" remained in place.

In the years that followed, the civil rights movement began to gain traction after the brutal murder of Emmett Till, who was falsely accused of "offending" a white woman, and his mother's courage in deciding to publicize not only his funeral but the scope of his injuries. Till's murder was followed by the Montgomery bus boycott, and the increasing ubiquity of television made it impossible to keep the violence against Southern Blacks out of view. Progress was made with the passage of the Civil Rights Act in 1964 and the Voting Rights Act in 1965, but of course it turned out the fight was just beginning. And the powers that be had no intention of losing.

CHAPTER 2

Impunity

James Eastland, the scion of a wealthy, powerful Mississippi plantation family, was elected to the United States Senate in 1942. He was named for his uncle, who had been murdered in an altercation in 1904, the year he was born. The hunting and lynching of the alleged murderer and the woman who ran with him were orchestrated by the younger Eastland's father, Woods Eastland. The man and woman Woods lynched were Luther Holbert and his wife.

While in the Senate, where he used his power to promote a virulently white supremacist agenda, Eastland, who continued to run his plantation with the labor of sharecroppers, was called "The Voice of the White South." In 1956 he became chair of the Judiciary Committee, which, under his leadership, was known as the graveyard of civil rights legislation. He was still chair of the Judiciary Committee when he retired in 1978, taking his unreconstructed Southern racism with him.

• • •

Ours is an ugly history full of depraved, barbaric, and inhumane behavior carried out by everyday people and encouraged or at least condoned by leaders at the highest levels of government. A denial of that history is a denial of our trauma.

Let's assume for the sake of argument that Robert E. Lee was a brilliant military strategist (he wasn't—he and his army were beaten decisively by superior military minds like Union generals William Tecumseh Sherman and Ulysses S. Grant). Let's assume that he was a good Christian man who worked hard after the Civil War to unite the country. Given certain indisputable facts about Lee's life, it's hard to see how any of that is relevant or makes him worthy of absolution.

First of all, Lee presided over a traitorous army whose mission was to destroy the United States for the purpose of protecting the right of the Southern states to continue to own and torture human beings. In the process of this failed secession, millions of soldiers on both sides suffered horribly under terrible conditions, and about 750,000 of them perished in battle and from disease.

Second, Lee enslaved people, despite claiming it was a "moral and political evil."

I think it however a greater evil to the white man than to the black race, & while my feelings are strongly enlisted in behalf of the latter, my sympathies are more strong for the former. The blacks are immeasurably better off here than in Africa, morally, socially & physically. The painful discipline they are undergoing, is necessary for their instruction as a race.

For Lee, the "painful discipline" included the practice of brining. In one instance, siblings Wesley and Mary Norris and a cousin of theirs, all three of whom had been "bequeathed" to Lee by his father-in-law with the expectation that they be emancipated within five years, were each given fifty lashes for attempting to run away to the North. Not satisfied that this punishment was sufficient, Lee ordered that their wounds be soaked with salt water.

Third, despite having written that he wished Blacks "no evil in the world," Lee broke up all but one of the families of enslaved people on his estate. Being separated from children, parents, siblings, and spouses was one of the most profound cruelties of slavery. After emancipation, freedmen and freedwomen did everything in their power to find their lost loved ones. Some kept up the search for decades, usually without success. The pain these separations caused was so great that it led one formerly enslaved man, Henry Bibb, to write in 1849, "If there was any one act of my life while a slave, that I have to lament over, it is that of being a father and a husband of slaves."

Whatever Lee's real or imagined accomplishments as a general of an army of traitors, he was a vile human being. That he was allowed to walk free after the war was a travesty. But he actually thrived, becoming president of Washington College, which was later renamed, in his honor, Washington and Lee. During his tenure as president, a chapter of the KKK was founded at the school, and Lee, not surprisingly, looked the other way.

According to U.S. constitutional law, Lee and the other leaders of the rebellion should have been hanged for treason or at the very least been made examples of. That former Confederate leaders were allowed not only to be rehabilitated but elevated was one of the reasons Lee's reputation has mutated into an utter fiction.

Robert E. Lee was a traitor to America who, as far as I can tell, never repented of his crimes against this country or against humanity.

After the war, he did lose the right to vote, and some of his property was confiscated and turned into Arlington National Cemetery. (It's worth noting that, unlike Black Americans, Lee's family was compensated for the property confiscated from Lee, ten years after his death.) Other than that, he was neither jailed nor punished. He petitioned to have his citizenship and voting rights restored but, thanks to the decency of Secretary of State William Seward, those requests were ignored.

In some ways, the North is just as responsible as the South for Lee's role in perpetuating the propaganda known as the Lost Cause, the myth that the South seceded as a rebuke to an overreaching federal government and had nothing to do with slavery. A great opportunity was missed when the Confederate battle flag, which stands for treason and human cruelty, did not come to be viewed with the same universal horror as the swastika is in Germany. Today, it is still proudly flown as a symbol of what some call "Southern pride," even though it is still, as the Southern Baptist Convention said in 2016, "a symbol of hatred, bigotry, and racism."

Slavery was legal and accepted throughout America, but it was not *universally* accepted, and even among enslavers it was believed to be an "evil," if a necessary one. While it is indisputable that Thomas Jefferson was an architect, author of the Declaration of Independence, founding father, and third president of the United States, he was also a man who enslaved more than six hundred people. He repeatedly raped Sally Hemings, whom he considered his property, starting when she was fourteen and he was forty-four. Despite the fact that Jefferson argued against race mixing because Black people were "inferior to the whites in the endowments both of body and mind," he fathered children, at least six, with Hemings. These children—his children—were also enslaved by him.

Do criminality, racism, and cruelty erase the achievements made during the tenure of a particular administration? No, but those things should force a conversation at least about the individual at the head of the administration. We expect a certain amount of hagiography, but regardless of his accomplishments, it's hard to reconcile Jefferson's stature as a "great" president or man with his disastrous assimilationist policy for Native Americans, his slaveholding, and his cruelty toward those enslaved human beings who, by virtue of his owning them as property, were entirely dependent on him. That an individual who championed democracy, republicanism, and individual rights, especially one with the power and influence Jefferson wielded, and especially the writer of the document that forcefully argued for equality and the "rights of man," would choose to own other human beings is important information to have. How an enslaver treated the enslaved also matters. There is no sliding scale when it comes to the crime against humanity that is slavery, but when that crime is exacerbated by acts of torture, rape, and brutality, those acts speak to an enslaver's character, whether such behavior was legal or not.

The need for and purpose of accountability are often obscured by revisionist history that hides or completely elides facts that might otherwise help us revise our assessments of people like Robert E. Lee and Thomas Jefferson. Only by clear, factual reckoning of history can we make more informed decisions about who we hold up as an example.

We want to identify with our leaders. At least retrospectively, we want to find things in them to admire, to emulate, even if they made mistakes—or perhaps because they made mistakes. But many of our founders and most of our presidents who are held in the highest esteem held repugnant views or committed horrible acts. Indeed, seventeen of the fifty-five delegates to the Constitutional Convention were enslavers, as were twelve of the first eighteen presidents.

The lack of accountability continued into the twentieth century, in sometimes flagrant and shocking ways.

President Gerald Ford is responsible for two of the worst pardons in American history, with an honorable mention for President Jimmy Carter.

In 1975, after 110 years had washed away Lee's sins and reinvented him as some kind of hero, the U.S. House of Representatives voted 407–10 to restore Lee's full rights of citizenship. A couple of weeks later, President Ford signed the resolution in order to correct an "oversight."

During the ceremony, Ford said:

> As a soldier, General Lee left his mark on military strategy. As a man, he stood as the symbol of valor and of duty. As an educator, he appealed to reason and learning to achieve understanding and to build a stronger nation. The course he chose after the war became a symbol to all those who had marched with him in the bitter years towards Appomattox. General Lee's character has been an example to succeeding generations, making the restoration of his citizenship an event in which every American can take pride.

I can only imagine how the descendants of the people he enslaved and of the Union soldiers who died because of him must have felt.

Three years later, in an equally gratuitous act of historical illiteracy, Jimmy Carter restored citizenship to the president of the Confederacy,

Jefferson Davis; doing so, he said, "completes the long process of reconciliation that has reunited our people following the tragic conflict between the states."

As historian Francis MacDonnell wrote, "The separate measures assured that the two deceased Confederates might legally hold office and serve jury duty."

Richard Nixon would provide the paradigm for what's come after him—the danger of allowing a candidate's attempt to steal (or succeed at stealing) an election to go unchallenged because it would "look bad." Once he's allowed in, there's a good chance he'll use his considerable (though illegitimate) powers to cover up the original crime and then go on to commit other crimes with impunity.

In a piece in *Politico*, "When a Candidate Conspired with a Foreign Power to Win an Election," on Nixon's successful plot to scuttle Lyndon Johnson's nascent peace talks with the Vietnamese just before the 1968 election, John A. Farrell dissects the details not just of the crime but of the successful efforts to keep Nixon's involvement in the theft of the election under wraps for over fifty years.

In October 1968, concerned that President Johnson's efforts to hold peace talks would bear fruit, Nixon ordered his future chief of staff, H. R. Haldeman, to find ways to sabotage them. He hoped that if Johnson failed to achieve a cease-fire before November, voters would punish the Democratic Party and its candidate, Hubert Humphrey, and reward the Republican candidate with a victory in the upcoming presidential election.

With polls narrowing, Nixon enlisted the help of Anna Chennault, a Washington hostess and lobbyist, to open a back channel to South Vietnamese president Nguyen Van Thieu. "Hold on," she told Thieu. "We are gonna win." In other words, scuttle the peace talks and, when Nixon is in office, we'll get you a better deal. Haldeman's notes at the time include this damning sentence: "Keep Anna Chennault working on SVN," which he wrote while on the phone with his boss.

Nixon may have thought that the proposed peace talks were a ploy to give the Democrats a boost ahead of Election Day, but Johnson and his team genuinely believed that there was potential for success. As Walt Rostow, Johnson's national security adviser, put it, "We have the best deal now we can get."

With transcripts of Chennault's phone calls to Saigon provided to him by the FBI, Johnson was convinced of Nixon's involvement. He said to Republican senator Everett Dirksen, "It's despicable. . . . We could stop the killing out there. But they've got this . . . new formula put in there—namely, wait on Nixon. And they're killing four or five hundred every day waiting on Nixon." And he added, "This is treason."

But there was no definitive proof of Nixon's involvement, and Johnson felt he couldn't risk revealing his surveillance of both Nixon and the South Vietnamese. He also had to factor in his concern about how the resulting scandal might affect efforts to end the war.

Nixon went on to win the 1968 election, despite his egregious violations of the Logan Act, which makes it a crime for unauthorized Americans to enter into negotiations with a foreign power. In other words, he cheated. The killing of Americans and Vietnamese continued for another seven years, the promising peace plan Johnson had been on the verge of securing unsalvageable. On Nixon's watch, twenty thousand more Americans and tens of thousands of Vietnamese, Cambodians, and Laotians died. It turns out he would face impeachment for the wrong crime.

• • •

Worried that Nixon could face criminal charges after his resignation due to the Watergate break-in and cover-up, Ford pardoned him on September 8, 1974, writing that "the tranquility to which this nation has been restored by the events of recent weeks could be irreparably lost." The decision was controversial at the time, and many critics accused Ford of making a "corrupt bargain." Despite Ford's protestations to the contrary, presidential historian Douglas Brinkley told *The New York Times* in September 2018 that Ford's pardon of Nixon "set a precedent that presidents are superhuman and not held to the rule of law like other people. [Pardons] are supposed to correct travesties of justice."

But time continues to heal all powerful white men's wounds. In 2001 Ford was presented with the John F. Kennedy Profile in Courage Award for "his courage in making a controversial decision of conscience to pardon former President Richard M. Nixon."

In her presentation of the award to the former president, Caroline Kennedy said, "For more than a quarter century, Gerald Ford proved to the people of Michigan, the Congress, and our nation that politics can be a noble profession. As president, he made a controversial decision of conscience to pardon former president Nixon and end the national trauma of Watergate. In doing so, he placed his love of country ahead of his own political future." And he also set the terrible precedent that, if you commit crimes while you are president, there will be no consequences. I think it's safe to say this is a precedent we have all come to regret.

It should not be lost on us that at the same ceremony, Congressman John Lewis, who literally *risked his life* in the fight against racial inequality, received the John F. Kennedy Profile in Courage Award for Lifetime Achievement.

· · ·

And the lack of accountability continued into the twenty-first century, well before Donald took office.

After his election, President Barack Obama indicated that he most likely would not authorize an investigation into the Bush administration's torture of terrorism suspects. Reasons Obama gave in an interview with NBC News included the desire to not seem vengeful (as if seeking justice for crimes that violated the Geneva Conventions could reasonably be said to constitute revenge); not spend the new administration's "time and energy rehashing the perceived sins of the old one"; appease the powers that be at the CIA, who strenuously opposed any inquiries into the torture program, in order to avoid making them feel like the administration was "looking over their shoulders"; and, the most misguided rationale of all, "to look forward as opposed to looking backward."

Obama's recalcitrance in this matter helped, in the words of Adam Serwer, writing for *The Atlantic* in March 2018, to "entrench a standard of accountability that stretches from beat cops to CIA officials, one in which breaking the law in the line of duty is unpunishable, but those suspected of a crime—particularly if Black, Muslim, or undocumented—can be subjected to unspeakable cruelty whether or not they are ultimately guilty." Failing to hold accountable those in whom a great deal of trust and power has been placed turns on its head the whole notion that "with great power comes great responsibility." In America, that is almost never true and, more consequentially, it is almost in diametric opposition to the truth of how things really work. The more power you have, the fewer consequences you face.

Like Ford, who failed to hold prior crimes to account, Obama committed two egregious mistakes in failing to hold prior crimes to account. In the United States during the two years between 2007 and 2009, the value of homes plummeted, the stock market crashed, and unemployment rose to 10 percent. All told, Americans lost $9.8 trillion in wealth, while stock market losses totaled $8 trillion, putting the entire global economy at risk of collapse.

The precipitating cause of this crisis was the bursting of the housing bubble, but other causes included a decades-long trend of banking industry deregulation, which opened up the opportunity for people who historically had not been able to afford conventional mortgages to be approved for riskier loans. From 2003 to 2007, these so-called subprime mortgages went from representing 6 percent to 14 percent of all mortgages. The increased availability of cheap mortgages led to an increased demand for housing, which peaked in 2006.

The catch was that, beginning in 2004, the Federal Reserve began raising interest rates, which most new homeowners had not expected. In 2003, the rate was 1 percent, but by 2006 it had climbed to 5.25 percent. As rates continued to rise, housing prices began to slide, until the debt owed on millions of new and refinanced mortgages was greater than the values of the homes themselves. Homeowners found themselves trapped between mortgage payments they could no longer afford and houses they could no longer sell. When the housing bubble burst, the stock market collapse quickly followed.

Lost income, lost productivity, and lost assets led to a loss of approximately seventy thousand dollars in lifetime income for every American. By 2010 there were a total of 3.8 million foreclosures. Some people recovered, but many never did, thanks in large part to the Obama administration's decision not to hold the banks accountable.

JPMorgan Chase and Bank of America paid thirteen billion and seventeen billion dollars in fines, respectively, yet Eric Holder's Justice Department claimed it could find no evidence of wrongdoing. Besides, as Holder said, these financial institutions had become so large that it was "difficult for us to prosecute them." The infamous "too big to fail" argument has led to a situation in which many Americans struggle within a system rigged against them and *for* the banks, which have gotten even bigger, gaining in excess of $2.4 trillion in the years since they almost destroyed the world's economy and actually did destroy the lives of countless people.

Some of the most egregious crimes in American history weren't crimes at the time or were sanctioned government policy, like the forced relocation of one hundred thousand Native Americans during Andrew Jackson's Trail of Tears and the domestic slave trade in the decades after the international slave trade was abolished. But it is only by confronting these atrocities, sanctioned or not, that we can put this country's history—and where it's led us—in perspective. By not having that information at our disposal, or by having it sanitized, we do ourselves a disservice. Even small acts of whitewashing skew history in a way that fails us. The website for Monticello, Jefferson's sprawling plantation, refers to him as a "patriarch of an extended family at Monticello, both white and black," which is an odd way of describing the enslaved children Sally Hemings bore him.

Such inquiries do not demonize those who make mistakes. But if we fail to ask the questions, we are likely to make more egregious mistakes because we don't acknowledge the original ones. We should not talk about the founders of this country without talking about which of them were enslavers, which ones actually supported the idea of owning other human beings, and yet we do. That's the first thing we should know about them, and then we can judge the rest accordingly.

Even Abraham Lincoln, considered our greatest president, struggled to accept the equality of Black Americans, despite believing they should be free. As Frederick Douglass remarked in his "Oration in Memory of Abraham Lincoln," "Viewed from the genuine abolition ground, Mr. Lincoln seemed tardy, cold, dull, and indifferent; but measuring him by the sentiment of his country, a sentiment he was bound as a statesman to consult, he was swift, zealous, radical, and determined." Franklin Delano Roosevelt allowed the internment of Japanese Americans during World War II because of rampant xenophobia that was aimed directly at American citizens who were of Japanese descent and looked like the enemy. His New Deal largely excluded Black Americans from the economic opportunities afforded white Americans, effectively shutting them out of the middle class. Racist policies pursued by many government organizations under his watch worsened the already bad problem of housing segregation, which forced Blacks into crowded, substandard living situations.

Failing to demand a reckoning for atrocities, even retrospectively, creates a situation in which we ensure such atrocities or crimes or transgressions will happen again. Failing to call them out is to condone them.

Ironically, the fear of being associated with past transgressions often leads to silence about them. As we see with child abuse, sexual assault, and mental illness, which often go unreported, shame can be a powerful silencer.

Failing to acknowledge the fact that the original sins have not been atoned for, acting as if the recompense is firmly in the past, adequate and complete, is to perpetuate the injustices and pave the way for future transgression and brutality. Cruelty and bigotry and white impunity are built into the system. And by remaining silent about historical truths, couching them in euphemisms, or rewriting them altogether, we ensure that the system will not change.

Abraham Lincoln's assassination was followed by the presidency of Andrew Johnson, who not only halted the momentum of Reconstruction but also seemed determined to undermine the very purpose for which the Civil War had been fought. Reconstruction was followed by the backlash of Jim Crow and the reenslavement of Blacks under the system of peonage; the Civil Rights Act of 1964 was followed by the backlash of the "war on drugs" and the resulting mass incarceration of Black men; Obama's presidency was followed by the backlash of Donald's "election" (which, even if history proves he didn't win on the merits, was much closer than it ever should have been).

In administration after administration and across centuries and decades, crimes—against decency, against democracy, and against humanity—have been committed by presidents, legislators at all levels of government, the judiciary, and ordinary Americans without punishment, reprisal, or justice for the victims. Then Donald came along and left all of them in the dust.

PART II

Here There Be Monsters

CHAPTER 3

American Carnage

I t's fitting that it rained on January 20, 2017. It's fitting that Donald would later lie about the rain. The gloom that emanated from his "American carnage" inauguration speech felt like a threat, a road map for his administration, not an assessment. This threat had been foreshadowed by his chilling pronouncement at the 2016 Republican convention: "I alone can fix it." I didn't take him seriously at the time (it was just Donald, after all), but people who understood the peril much better than I—people like Ruth Ben-Ghiat, Sarah Kendzior, and Malcolm Nance— certainly did.

That he would kick off his first full day in office with a lie about the size of the inauguration crowd suited both the man and the occasion. The lies themselves, which seemed to grow exponentially over time and went largely unchallenged by his own party, came to feel like assaults—on our sense of basic human decency, our ideas about America's place in the world, the belief that our system of checks and balances would see us through. Going forward, we should have—but didn't—expect to be lied to and gaslighted at every turn.

Once in office, Donald would push the envelope and wait to see how much he could get away with, as he had always done. And if he *did* get away with it, he'd push even further, because there was no bottom to him—there never had been. What remained to be determined was whether or not the Republican Party, which had mostly lined up behind him during the general election, didn't have a bottom, either. With the exception of Donald's being thwarted in his effort to scuttle the Afford-able Care Act, thanks to the "no" votes of three Republican senators, there are precious few instances in which he didn't get his way, whether in setting policy, in stealing from the Treasury to enrich himself, or in inflicting as much pain as possible on as many people as possible.

For the first two years of his term, the worst among us—the nativists, the nationalists, the unrepentant white supremacists—were represented by Republicans who controlled 100 percent of the federal government. This "worst" exists in any society, but one of the purposes of liberal democracy is to contain them and their ability to spread their hatred. Between 2017 and 2019, however, their racism, misogyny, and homophobia metastasized. The general public's misplaced belief in the inherent soundness of the system and in the good faith of those operating in it created an opportunity for the malignant forces that had gone underground or been pushed to the edges of our civil society to surge and take center stage. The Republican base, their views validated and championed by those at the highest levels of govern-ment, became mobilized in a way they hadn't been in decades. The message to Black Americans in particular was clear: the worst of us will always be better than the best of you, and sixty-two million Donald voters had chosen exactly the right person to make that argument.

The impetus for the Women's March that took place in Washington as well as in cities around the country and the world the day after Donald's inauguration was to force an examination of the grievous wound that had been inflicted on half of the population by the election of a man who appeared to have won in part because of, not in spite of, his numerous alleged assaults on women. In retrospect, the march also seems like a last-gasp attempt at collective healing that couldn't be sustained, because you cannot heal while you're still being traumatized. After the march, the expectation, or the hope, was that the Republican Party would stop him, but having hope is itself a kind of normalization; if you have hope, you have an expectation that something will change. This misled many people, because nothing did change. Besides, the people who could have acted, if not to oust him (that was a pipe dream) then at least to rein in his worst impulses, benefited too much from having at their disposal somebody as incompetent, grasping, and uninterested in the job as Donald. It was a great stroke of luck for them to have found somebody so manipulable—even more so than George W. Bush—in the Oval Office.

As they had been doing for decades, the Democrats in power continued to misread the character of the Republican Party and its extreme rightward shift. They failed to realize the rules no longer applied; that, indeed, the rule book had been doused in gasoline and lit on fire.

At times it seemed like one of Donald's main motives was to demoralize those who hadn't supported him. Almost everything was designed to underscore the powerlessness of the Democratic opposition, which, after November 2016, controlled not one lever of power.

The attacks on the press were deliberate—as Lesley Stahl reported that Donald said to her in their May 2018 interview: "I do it to demean you and discredit you, so no one will believe you." And they were made worse by the fact that many journalists and news outlets, despite being labeled time and again as "fake news" and "the enemy of the people," continued to normalize Donald's behavior, as if his becoming presidential was just around the corner, giving him credit for simply reading off a teleprompter without incident.

During the campaign, ratings kept the media from asking Donald serious questions. At one point he claimed, absurdly, to know more about ISIS than the "generals." No one bothered to ask how he knew more or what exactly he knew. Donald's racism, his use of incendiary language, his shredding of norms, his breathtaking and obvious ignorance, and his arrogance in thinking he didn't need to make sense were all taken for granted. As a candidate, the Republican nominee repeatedly demonstrated he had not read, let alone *understood,* the foundational document of the country he sought to lead, but the media rarely called him on it. True, it's never been required of candidates, but no candidate in the history of American presidential elections has ever demonstrated such ignorance of basic civics. Even if the media did on occasion challenge Donald during the primaries and general election, they lent his campaign an aura of importance he hadn't earned by training their cameras on empty podiums and planes idling on the tarmac, as if *waiting* for Donald was more important than listening to anything any of the other candidates had to say. The grievous disparity between how he and his opponents were treated—particularly in the general election—was ignored or downplayed.

Out of "respect" for the office, or a desire for continued access to the White House, reporters kept asking the wrong questions. For example, instead of asking which Democrat could beat Donald in 2020, they should have been asking, Why is someone so unfit, who lies to the American people multiple times each day, who constantly betrays his oath to uphold and defend the Constitution, and who puts his own self-interest above the country's national security interests in increasingly alarming ways, being allowed to run?

During his time in office, the media failed to put the actions of his administration in particular and those of the Republican Party in general in their proper context. Donald wasn't just incompetent, laughable, and cruel—though he was all of those—he was actively laying the groundwork, through his rhetoric, his policies, and his perversion of democratic norms and institutions, for autocracy. The Republican Party wasn't simply wielding its power to push through a mandate in the furtherance of democracy; it was engaging in antidemocratic, counter-majoritarian tactics that aligned with their goal of clinging to power and establishing minority rule. Both the executive and legislative branches were trending toward fascism, but a mainstream media that had been reluctant to call a liar a liar or a racist a racist during the first three years Donald was in the Oval Office certainly couldn't be counted on to find the language necessary to describe the reality of our increasingly fraught political moment.

The politically motivated attacks inspired by Donald's rhetoric and his example contributed to the growing sense of chaos. From the mass murder at two mosques in New Zealand in which fifty-one people were killed to the attack at the Tree of Life synagogue in Pittsburgh in which eleven people were killed to the El Paso shooting in which twenty-three people were killed, a line can be drawn to Donald's unrestrained anti-Semitism and xenophobia, demonstrated by his talk of Mexican "hordes" and his description of neo-Nazis as "fine people." He tweeted his vitriol and used the most powerful platform on the planet to demonize one group and support the other. Putting it out there so blatantly had the counterintuitive effect of making his views more acceptable to tens of millions of people. If what he was saying was so bad, wouldn't he keep it hidden?

Women were targeted. Muslims were targeted. The LGBTQ community was targeted. Poor people were targeted. Puerto Ricans were targeted. And then children were targeted, too.

The cruelty of the first three years reached its peak with the implementation of the child separation policy (so-called zero tolerance), which was adopted in April 2018. Every other morally bankrupt act that had gone before—from the travel ban of several majority-Muslim countries to the exclusion of new transgender troops from the military to the blocking of Syrian refugees—suddenly seemed a prelude to this particular horror. It felt like the school shooting at Sandy Hook Elementary School that claimed the lives of twenty first graders, with this difference: our government was the perpetrator. In justifying the policy, Attorney General Jeff Sessions said, "If you don't want your child separated, then don't bring them across the border illegally. It's not our fault that somebody does that." It was the language of the abuser. The U.S. government kidnapped the children, even those who had family living legally in the United States, put them into concentration camps, and then, due to incompetence, carelessness, or depravity, was unable to unite many of these children with their families because the government hadn't bothered to keep track of them.

Next, he went after our institutions.

On September 1, 2019, Donald tweeted that Hurricane Dorian was heading toward Alabama. It was a mistake—a simple mistake that anybody could have made. When the Birmingham office of the National Weather Service corrected him in a tweet ("Alabama will NOT see any impacts from Dorian"), his pathological aversion to admitting he's wrong prompted an absurd doubling down. He created false evidence, revising a map of the hurricane's path with, of all things, a Sharpie. It was obvious and embarrassing and most people didn't take it (or him) seriously. Some Alabamans might have done so, however, in which case they thought Dorian could be headed their way. But it wasn't so, and in the end his lie was harmless.

Or was it? What if the opposite scenario had played out, and a dangerous hurricane *had been* headed Alabama's way and Donald had mistakenly tweeted that Alabama would be spared? What if he doubled down on *this* claim when corrected and then changed the map to *exclude* Alabama from the hurricane's path? Would some residents, believing they were out of danger, have failed to prepare? What if people had died because, instead of trusting the experts, they listened instead to the man in the Oval Office? The National Oceanic and Atmospheric Administration (NOAA), up until then an elite government agency, didn't do itself any favors when five days later it released an unsigned statement that read, in part, "Hurricane Dorian could impact Alabama," which backed up Donald's lie and undercut the National Weather Service's truth. The question is, why?

Almost everything that Donald did from the 2017 inauguration on— the gratuitous cruelty, the international embarrassments, the lawbreaking, the bullying, the endless trips to his golf courses, and the juvenile tweeting—took its toll on us both as individuals and as a society. Our political divide seemed to be widening past the point of coherence, but beyond that, none of what was happening seemed to threaten the fundamental landscape of American democracy. No, this wasn't where the real damage was being done.

In retrospect, the stories that took up most of our attention (and sapped most of our strength) did exactly what they were meant to do: keep us from focusing on what was really happening below the radar. The contours of our government were shifting. Only the most practiced (or obsessed) observer could have pieced together the fact that the on-slaught of foreign policy blunders and lies and the displays of incompetence and nepotism and grifting were distracting us from the real threat this administration posed—the systematic dismantling of the very institutions put in place to protect us when people like Donald manage to ascend to power.

Fragile systems bend toward the dysfunction of the most psychologically disordered member of the system, especially if that person is disproportionately powerful. America's institutions were designed to be impervious to the depredations of any one individual, regardless of how dysfunctional he might be, but in a country that relies so heavily upon traditions and norms, the Senate, cabinet members, and advisers need to act as safeguards, not accomplices. When they fail to—or choose not to—rein in the dysfunctional individual, he (with assistance from his enablers) is left with all of the resources of his position at his disposal to pervert every institution he controls until they come to amplify and exemplify the worst of him.

At literally every single cabinet-level agency in our government there was significant disruption during the four years of Donald's administration at both the structural and human level. It's not as if these agencies had become newly vulnerable when Donald entered the Oval Office, and it's not as if Donald was the first White House occupant to co-opt the Department of Justice for his own purposes. He was just the first one lucky enough to have his party in complete control of the government and, thanks in part to looming demographic irrelevance, desperate enough to let him break or exploit whatever he could get his hands on as long as the party got its originalist judges, its tax cuts, its voter suppression, and its gerrymandering. Donald was the Republican Party without the pretense.

Barack Obama and George W. Bush could have bent Justice and State to do their bidding if they'd been so inclined, if it had occurred to them to try as long as their party was in power and willing to be complicit. The danger going forward is that the path has already been walked. All it's going to take to complete the destruction is for another authoritarian to get into the White House with a legislative branch that's willing to do his bidding.

What many of us didn't realize is that most of our government is based on the belief that antiquated concepts like honor and shame will sufficiently motivate our elected officials to follow precedent. As incompetent as most of the people in Donald's inner circle were, there were some who knew how to suss out the weaknesses in the system and were willing to exploit them. It's easy to break shit, especially when you think doing so will benefit you. Donald's entire career has demonstrated that he is much better at tearing things down than he is at building them, so it should have come as no surprise that his administration would be as well.

The unique threat Donald posed was made worse by his administration's almost total lack of transparency. It would be up to the media, the courts, and Congress to keep us informed and protect us from executive branch overreach. From the inauguration on, those institutions largely failed us (Congress most of all), either by failing to take Donald seriously or portray his actions in a straightforward way or through their willingness to exploit him for their own purposes (ratings, ideology, or raw power), no matter the cost to the American people or the American experiment.

So while no one was keeping tabs, Donald was free to treat cabinet nominations as ambassadorships, a way to pay back cronies and allies. There's no other explanation for former Texas governor Rick Perry, neurosurgeon Ben Carson, or wealthy person (and sister of mercenary Erik Prince) Betsy DeVos to have been placed at the departments of

Energy, Housing and Urban Development, and Education, respectively. None of them had relevant experience. Perry had previously run for president on a platform that would have included eliminating the Department of Energy if he could have remembered its name. In the case of DeVos, her role as a staunch advocate for school choice (teachers unions were critical of her nomination) and her public pronouncements on the relationship between schools and Christianity (she described education activism and reform efforts as means to "advance God's Kingdom") were even more alarming. A comprehensive report by Becca Damante, posted on the online forum Just Security in September 2020, found that fifteen officials in Donald's administration in "acting" positions held their positions illegally. Other positions were kept vacant on purpose. It's a lot easier to push through your agenda and get away with repurposing the cabinet-level departments if you're willing to break the law and nobody bothers to stop you.

The greatest damage done during Donald's tenure, though, was at agencies where the people put in charge deliberately changed the culture and the mission of the organizations they led. In terms of short-term consequences and long-lasting impact, the most negatively affected were the Department of State and the Department of Justice. (The Centers for Disease Control and Prevention also suffered under the administration, but the extent to which this was the case wasn't revealed until COVID hit.)

The Department of Justice mission statement is straightforward enough: "to enforce the law and defend the interests of the United States according to the law; to ensure public safety against threats foreign and domestic; to provide federal leadership in preventing and controlling crime; to seek just punishment for those guilty of unlawful behavior; and to ensure fair and impartial administration of justice for all Americans."

It says nothing about defending the interests of any particular individual. Nonetheless, Donald, forever in search of his Roy Cohn, made the assumption that people would do his bidding even if they worked for the government and not for him. When James Comey at the FBI and Sally Yates at Justice failed that test, they were both dismissed.

Jeff Sessions seemed the perfect guy to put in charge of the Department of Justice—in February 2016 he had been the first senator to endorse Donald, a potentially risky move politically. But getting the job had been his goal all along, and it paid off. In 1986, when Sessions had been picked by President Ronald Reagan for a judgeship in the U.S. District Court for the Southern District of Alabama, things hadn't gone as smoothly. His nomination couldn't get out of the Judiciary Committee. The bipartisan vote was 10–8 to oppose recommending him to the full Senate for a vote. Numerous charges of racism along with his shoddy record on civil rights torpedoed his chances. Attorney General Edwin Meese called the committee's failure to approve the nomination "an appalling surrender" to the politics of ideology, as if antiracism is an ideology that shouldn't be submitted to. In any case, the judgeship went to somebody else.

This time the Sessions nomination for the position of attorney general made it through the Judiciary Committee and a bitter fight in the Senate ensued. Many of the same accusations of racism from the 1986 nomination were raised, and some of them, including a letter by Coretta Scott King that Senator Elizabeth Warren attempted to read into the record, were silenced by then majority leader Mitch McConnell. The final vote to confirm Sessions was 52–47, almost entirely along party lines, with the exception of Joe Manchin, Democrat from West Virginia, who also voted aye. Racism was no longer an obstacle in today's Republican Party.

Not surprisingly, Sessions would curtail the use of consent decrees, an important tool in helping the Department of Justice enforce civil rights. The DOJ was founded in 1870, and one of its original mandates was to protect freedmen and freedwomen from potential abuses after the Civil War. Sessions was making it harder for his own department to do the important work of ensuring police integrity, in direct contradiction of that mandate.

Sessions made one mistake, however—he forgot where his loyalties lay. After it was revealed he had met twice with Russian ambassador Sergey Kislyak during the 2016 campaign (contradicting a sworn statement he had made during his confirmation hearing), Sessions recused himself from the investigation of the serious allegations that Russia had interfered with the election in order to swing the results in Donald's favor and that Donald and his advisers had eagerly accepted that help. As a result, Robert Mueller was appointed Special Counsel, prompting Donald to exclaim, according to the report Mueller eventually wrote, "Oh my God. This is terrible. This is the end of my presidency. I'm fucked." Although Donald didn't accept Sessions's proffered resignation, he never got over what he deemed a betrayal—he had wanted a loyalist handling the Russia investigation and Sessions failed to deliver. Donald continued to torment his attorney general, largely via tweet, until Sessions resigned in November 2018 in order to run unsuccessfully for his old senate seat.

After decades of searching (and three months of Acting Attorney General Matthew Whitaker), Donald finally found his Roy Cohn in the person of one William Barr. Barr made it clear even before taking office where his allegiance would lie when he sent an unsolicited memo to Deputy Attorney General Rod Rosenstein spelling out his ideas regarding obstruction of justice as they pertained to the Mueller probe. The document read more like an audition than anything else, so it's not surprising that Donald, desperate to impede, if not entirely crush, the investigation into his alleged conspiracy with a hostile foreign power, gave Barr the part.

Barr made no pretense at objectivity while in office. The list of his most egregious betrayals of the Department of Justice is long. It includes spiking whistleblower complaints; attempting to prosecute Donald's political enemies; attempting to take over Donald's defense in the E. Jean Carroll defamation suit because Donald was, according to court papers filed by the DOJ, acting in his "official capacity" when he denied her accusation that he had raped her; and appointing U.S. Attorney for Connecticut John Durham to investigate the *origins* of the FBI probe into Russian interference in the 2016 election (investigating the investigators). Barr's most consequential action came just before the release of the redacted Mueller report, when he claimed, falsely, that no conspiracy between the Trump campaign and Russian officials had been uncovered and no conclusion had been reached by Mueller and his team regarding the obstruction of justice charge. Mueller forcefully rejected this characterization in a private letter to Barr that was subsequently shared with *The Washington Post*, but the damage was done.

While the DOJ took stances against the protection of voting rights and against a university's race-conscious admissions policies, Barr took no interest in investigating claims of voter suppression. He also ignored the increasing threat of white supremacist domestic terrorism, focusing his concern instead, as he said during remarks at the University of Notre Dame law school, on the "militant secularists" behind a "campaign to destroy the traditional moral order," which, as far as I know, is not something that exists.

Donald Ayer, a former deputy attorney general in the George H. W. Bush administration, said Barr, who had worked with him, "poses the greatest threat, in my lifetime, to our rule of law and to public trust in it."

After George Floyd's murder in May 2020 and the Black Lives Matter protests that followed, Barr announced his intention to pursue an "independent investigation into possible violations of federal civil rights laws" in the killing of Floyd. Barr's promise rang hollow given the egregious failures of his department's Civil Rights Division to pursue cases of racial discrimination. As it turned out, the DOJ planned to investigate Derek Chauvin's murder of George Floyd independent of any review of corrupt practices and abuse within the Minneapolis police department, extending the practice of curtailing the use of consent decrees meant to ensure police integrity started by Jeff Sessions back in 2018.

Instead of investigating corrupt police practices, Barr focused on suppressing protests, or at least the kind of protests of which he did not approve. He made no effort to intervene in or investigate the mobs of heavily armed white men storming state capitols in order to intimidate state governments into easing COVID restrictions.

After Barr came to the conclusion that the Black Lives Matter protesters were not peaceful, he sanctioned, if not directly ordered, the use of pepper spray and rubber bullets, as well as the deployment of what appeared to be unidentified storm troopers in Portland, Oregon. When you conceptualize your interactions as "dominating the battle space" (as Secretary of Defense Mark Esper did at the time), your approach will be influenced by that framing, even if the people you end up assaulting are simply exercising their First Amendment rights.

Until Barr ran the DOJ, its Civil Rights Division had taken the lead on addressing affirmative action, segregation, predatory lending, and voting rights. Under his and Sessions's leadership, the message being sent by the Trump administration was that, in the words of Vanita Gupta, President Biden's associate attorney general, "civil rights enforcement is superfluous and can be easily cut. At worst, it really is part of a systematic agenda to roll back civil rights." In the words of Kristen Clarke, the new head of the Civil Rights Division under President Biden, "No administration has done more to obstruct and defy the mission of the division in its 63-year existence."

It is worth noting that Jeff Sessions, a racist who opposes civil rights and whose extreme views previously cost him a federal judgeship, received fifty-one votes from Republicans in his confirmation as attorney general in 2017. Kristen Clarke, who has dedicated her professional life to combating racism and defending civil rights, received only one Republican vote for her confirmation in 2021.

It may be a unique accomplishment in the history of American government that two of the worst, if not *the* two worst, secretaries of state came out of the same administration. Rex Tillerson, the former ExxonMobil CEO, who served from 2017 to 2018, and Mike Pompeo, the former director of the CIA, who served out the rest of Donald's only term, both richly deserve the honor. Ironically, they achieved this distinction by following very different paths—Tillerson because he was never able to forge an alliance with Donald or the administration, and Pompeo because there was no daylight between him and his boss.

It is impossible to know what Tillerson's motives were for wanting to be secretary of state, and it's impossible to know what his agenda was. In his one year at State, he exerted no influence in the administration and accomplished nothing of note. He did, however, oversee the greatest depletion of expertise and experience in the department's history—there were mass resignations, the number of new applicants plummeted, and the core of career diplomats was gutted when 60 percent of them left. Only about 40 percent of political appointees were confirmed, while important positions, like ambassador to South Korea and assistant secretaries supervising vital regions like Asia and the Middle East, were left unfilled. Altogether, these unfathomable staffing changes destroyed morale and weakened the State Department for a "generation," according to George Washington University's Elizabeth Saunders as quoted in a November 2017 piece in *Vox*.

Continuity of personnel is crucial to preserving institutional memory, and, whether he intended this explicitly or not, Tillerson endangered that continuity while also undermining the core mission of diplomacy. Without diplomacy the default becomes aggression, which unfortunately suited his successor, Pompeo, perfectly.

If his leadership abilities had been commensurate with his inflated sense of self, Pompeo might have been able to turn things around at State. As it was, the thin-skinned and belligerent secretary took a muscular approach when dealing with our allies and adversaries alike. At the end of Pompeo's tenure, North Korea had more nuclear weapons (despite Donald's claim of their great love for each other, Kim Jong-Un did not agree to adhere to the 2005 pledge to give up his nation's nuclear program) and Iran was closer to building one. Pompeo and his style were so unpopular abroad that he had to cancel his January 2021 "victory" lap in Europe because nobody wanted to meet with him.

Tillerson and Pompeo both had a negative and far-reaching impact on the State Department, but the real reason America's standing in the world fell further and faster than it ever had was down to Donald. His duplicity, double-dealing, and inability to see things from any perspective other than his own made our allies wary and put our adversaries on notice—Donald could be flattered and baited into doing their bidding.

To what extent these institutions recover under the Biden administration and beyond is yet to be seen. The question is how do we prevent such devastation from happening again?

Donald's unilateral withdrawal from the Joint Comprehensive Plan of Action—the Iran nuclear deal—and the Paris Climate Accord undermined the good faith we had built up among our allies over decades and resulted in a loss of trust that still plagues us.

As Mieke Eoyang, the deputy assistant secretary of defense for cyber policy in the Biden administration, points out, by looking at Donald's foreign policy approach through the lens of "his selfishness and disregard for the truth," we see that his attempts to try to make our national security personnel loyal to his personal interests and "his erratic nature have undermined other countries' ability to trust America's word in treaties."

On December 18, 2019, the House voted almost entirely along party lines to impeach Donald for obstruction of justice and abuse of power after it came to light that he had pressured Ukrainian president Volodymyr Zelensky into finding dirt on his presumed opponent in the 2020 election in exchange for releasing desperately needed aid. This violation of his oath of office was compounded by the fact that Donald essentially stonewalled the House inquiry into this event by instructing officials in his administration to ignore subpoenas and refuse to hand over documents.

Before the Senate trial even began, Majority Leader Mitch McConnell made it clear that it would be a travesty. "I'm not an impartial juror," he said. "This is a political process. There is not anything judicial about it. Impeachment is a political decision." Lindsey Graham, senator from South Carolina, who had been sucking up to Donald since the inauguration despite having said during the primary, "I think he's a kook. I think he's crazy. I think he's unfit for office," followed McConnell's lead: "I am trying to give a pretty clear signal I have made up my mind. I'm not trying to pretend to be a fair juror here. . . . I will do everything I can to make [the impeachment trial] die quickly." The Republican majority proceeded to do just that when on January 31, 2020, the Senate voted 51–49 not to allow witnesses to testify. Five days later Donald was acquitted. The vote was 52–48 to acquit on the abuse of power charge and 53–47 to acquit on the obstruction of Congress charge.

Ominously, Susan Collins, Republican senator from Maine, said after the acquittal, "I believe that the president has learned from this case. The president has been impeached. That's a pretty big lesson." She wasn't wrong, of course, but the lesson Donald learned wasn't the lesson Collins presumably had in mind.

The vote, though predictable, was yet another blow. After three years, we were already beaten down.

And then came the Plague.

CHAPTER 4

Abandon All Hope Ye Who Enter Here

In early 2020, my uncle Donald made the following comments:

"It's also more deadly than even your strenuous flus. This is deadly stuff."

"WE CANNOT LET THE CURE BE WORSE THAN THE PROBLEM ITSELF."

Unfortunately, the first was made privately in a February interview with Bob Woodward, in which he also said, "I wanted to always play it down. I still like playing it down, because I don't want to create a panic." The one written in all caps was a tweet to his tens of millions of followers posted on March 22. The public would not learn about the Woodward conversation until September.

In early February, Donald had just emerged unscathed from his first impeachment trial over his attempt to strong-arm the new president of Ukraine in the summer of 2019 into finding dirt on Joe Biden, whom he

deemed his greatest threat in the 2020 presidential election. With his acquittal, and the tacit go-ahead from the Republican majority in Congress
to use the (illegal) assistance of foreign powers—through coercion or
by simply asking, "Russia, if you're listening"—he turned his attention
full throttle to crafting his reelection campaign.

A few days before the tweet, I was watching with growing horror,
from afar, the chaos in Italy, where overwhelmed hospitals were having
to ration care. I tried to fend off the belief that such devastation could
happen here, that we would *allow* it to happen here, but finally gave in
to the reality that of course we would allow it to happen here—Donald
was in charge.

Almost overnight, the growing dread became an intimate terror that
disrupted sleep and altered my—and our—very experience of time. I
learned that I had been in contact with two people who came down with
serious cases of COVID, so I was separated from my daughter, who had
just been sent home from her abruptly shuttered college, by two flights
of stairs and hastily hung plastic sheeting that I'd bought in a panic at
our local Ace Hardware store. During the two weeks I was stuck in
my basement quarantining, it was hard to process the news that painful death by suffocation awaited far too many people. I thought often
of my father, because just like him, hundreds and then thousands of
people were dying without anybody who loved them present to hold
their hand.

Nassau County, where I lived, had the third-worst rate of COVID
infections, hospitalizations, and deaths in the country, and eventually the
world, following only New York City and Westchester County. From
our vantage point, the "problem" Donald referenced was the out-of-
control life-threatening virus and the mass death it was causing. My
friends in Manhattan described the nonstop blare of ambulance sirens

twenty-four hours a day, and the unsettling hum of refrigerated trucks lined up outside of hospitals, morgues, and funeral homes to hold the overflow of the dead.

It was hard to see how any cure could be worse.

The only upside was the sense that this emergency couldn't possibly last for more than a month or two. We didn't know it, of course, but we were nowhere near the end. It was only going to get worse. Then it was going to get worse than that.

The growing nightmare of climate change and our having put someone in the Oval Office who claimed "I don't believe it" at a crucial point of no return had already made me wonder if the planet was trying to get rid of us; now I was sure. You can debate religion or economic policy. But debating climate change and COVID-19 is tantamount to debating gravity or evolution. What you believe in those contexts is irrelevant because climate change and COVID-19 will continue to exist, ravaging our planet and our populations, whether you believe in them or not.

It had been a century since the last major pandemic—why now? Why couldn't it have happened during the Obama administration, one of the most competent in modern history? Obama's team had already written a pandemic playbook in 2016, designed to develop a coordinated U.S. government response to "high-consequence emerging disease threat anywhere in the world." In other words, it would prepare us for something like the SARS-CoV-2 pandemic. One of the first things Donald's team did when they took over the White House was to throw the playbook out. Mitch McConnell claimed they'd received no briefings or information of any kind, but this was far from the truth. In an interview with CNN, Jeremy Konyndyk, a member of Obama's Ebola response team, said, "They [the new administration] were extensively briefed, to the extent that they paid attention to these things during the transition."

If Hillary Clinton, the winner of the popular vote in 2016, had been in office when the coronavirus arrived, she would have pulled out all the stops to contain it. *Anybody else but Donald* would have. And there are three things anybody else would *not* have done: politicize lifesaving measures like wearing a mask; set up a false dichotomy between the economy and the value of human life; and make the calculation that endangering lives and eventually killing hundreds of thousands of people was a winning campaign strategy. On Memorial Day 2020, the White House ordered flags lowered to half-staff, but that was its only gesture of recognition, a pale shadow of solidarity.

As the year of COVID unfolded, it became clear that we were being betrayed by our own federal government. In some cases, we were also betrayed by our neighbors, people whose dangerous beliefs had previously been contained at the margins of society but had now been brought to the forefront and empowered. With Donald's explicit encouragement—"LIBERATE MICHIGAN! LIBERATE MINNESOTA!"—they wielded assault weapons at statehouses all over the country in the name of reclaiming their freedom from restrictions intended to save their lives, threatening lawmakers and spreading the virus. Their rights were unbound from responsibility to anything but their own misguided self-interest.

Donald's behavior functionally lacked empathy and stemmed from his fear of being associated with weakness. Increased testing would reveal the scope of the situation. In his mind, this would undermine his public and private belief that none of it was his responsibility. As he had in the three years prior, he lied, created chaos, and sought to divide us in ways we didn't see coming.

The irony is that through his inaction and the ensuing effort to cover it up, he *became* responsible for everything that has followed: the collapse of the economy, the fraying of our social fabric, and mass death.

In 2017, Donald gifted corporations with billions of dollars in tax cuts, which was touted as freeing up money for investment in more jobs, but was actually used for stock buybacks that increased stockholder wealth and did nothing for workers. Three years later, the Paycheck Protection Program was designed to throw even more money at corporations, while Republicans in Congress seemed intent on leaving the vast majority of Americans, including "essential" workers who risked their lives in order to provide services so the rest of us could stay safely home, out in the cold. People who had done their best and still had to live without a safety net when their jobs vanished as businesses shuttered were told that, even during a global pandemic, giving them a subsistence wage wasn't possible because it would encourage an unseemly dependence on the government. That was called "socialism" or "welfare." That the tax cuts and payroll bailout were corporate welfare was never discussed. The message was clear: the economy needed to open and the lives of workers were expendable. Donald ordered the meatpacking plants to stay open, despite the out-of-control rates of infection there. At the time, it was hard not to think that this was less incompetent than willful. As the months passed, plenty of evidence surfaced that it was all done on purpose.

With a week to go before the 2020 presidential election, White House Chief of Staff Mark Meadows said, "We're not going to control the pandemic. We are going to control the fact that we get vaccines, therapeutics, and other mitigations." It was a startling admission, but Meadows was simply putting into words what the administration had made clear with its actions all along—it would do nothing to encourage the American people to take steps that, according to officials in their own government, would mitigate the spread of the coronavirus. Donald, for his part, deliberately put people in danger at his crowded masks-optional rallies because, as he proclaimed, "we live in a free society." His need for attention and adulation was far more important than his followers' safety or lives. For the twenty-first-century Republican Party as led by Donald and his enablers, freedom—to own guns or flout pandemic regulations—came to mean doing whatever you want regardless of the consequences to other people. This impulse, more than anything, is what Donald had tapped into over the course of his single term in the Oval Office.

Laurie Garrett, a Pulitzer Prize–winning science journalist, puts this trend, as exemplified by the Trump administration's response to the coronavirus, in its proper context: the Republican Party's long-standing desire to shrink the federal government and eliminate its regulatory capacity. This included drastically downsizing the U.S. Public Health Service, thereby short-circuiting its ability to protect the health and safety of the American people.

It was all so unnecessary. Nobody would have bolted from Donald's base if he had embraced a commonsense approach to COVID. Tens of thousands of lives would have been spared, and the economy, after a short-term hit, would have bounced back. His most deranged supporters would have hailed him as a hero—and a lot of his detractors would have, too. But Donald is constitutionally incapable of leading. He is constitutionally incapable of making the right choice if in any way, real or imagined, doing so might conflict with his self-interest. Because COVID hit blue states first and was found to affect communities of color disproportionately, it was even easier for him to make that choice. It also ensured that his base would embrace the China-virus-is-a-hoax narrative, because it reinforced their belief in white supremacy and catered to their own need for divisiveness.

It was Donald's conscious choice to stand aside and do nothing while this virus invaded our country, ravaging our bodies, our communities, and our economy. States were forced to compete with one another to buy vital supplies from private contractors, but adding insult to injury, Donald's administration then intercepted and commandeered those supplies so FEMA could distribute them back to private contractors who resold them at a profit while state governments were struggling to keep the lights on as their tax base shriveled.

On August 3, 2020, a day before the United States surpassed 150,000 deaths from COVID, Donald's interview with Axios reporter Jonathan Swan aired on HBO. "It is what it is," he said after Swan pointed out that a thousand Americans were dying every day. That was a popular expression in my family, and hearing it sent a chill down my spine. Whenever my grandfather, my aunt, or one of my uncles had said it, it was always with a cruel indifference to somebody else in despair. Donald had said it to me at my grandparents' house in Queens when I'd asked why my grandfather insisted that my father's ashes were to be buried in the family plot instead of scattered off the coast of Montauk, as he'd wanted. "It is what it is, honeybunch."

In the fall, the administration started to present the incremental gains in the monthly jobs report as a sign the economy was growing, when in actuality it was slowly recovering the millions of jobs that it had hemorrhaged in the spring.

The abysmal pandemic response was a failure of leadership and a dereliction of duty that demanded Donald's removal from office. It was his enablers' conscious choice to keep him there and allow the devastation to continue.

As for the rest of us, it simply became too much to challenge every single one of his transgressions.

On July 17, 2020, Donald had told Fox News host Chris Wallace, "I don't agree with the statement that if everybody wears a mask, everything disappears." No, because giving credit to a piece of cloth would somehow take something away from him.

This is not about being unlucky enough to live in a time when a pandemic occurred, it's about the fact that the pandemic was allowed to worsen and grow. In all likelihood, nobody could have prevented the pandemic from starting, but so many lives were willfully sacrificed on the altar of Donald's reelection campaign, and the economy was allowed to fail for most of us because it succeeded for the very, very few, netting more than a trillion dollars for American billionaires as the stock market soared while millions of wage earners lost their jobs and had to resort to food banks to feed their families. It's impossible to say how Donald would have reacted if the stock market had been unaffected by the early warnings about COVID, but once he made the link between the virus and the Dow Jones Industrial Average—the only economic indicator that has ever mattered to him—he would continue to associate speaking honestly about COVID with an adverse impact on the economy.

As soon as he made the determination, which was breathtakingly stupid and cynical, that the economy was much more important than people's health, the economy and COVID became detached from each other in a way that they never should have been.

As another bogus justification for opening up the economy while COVID was still raging, Donald said, "My administration is committed to preventing the tragedy of suicide, ending the opioid crisis, and improving mental and behavioral health. . . . The pandemic has also exacerbated mental and behavioral-health conditions as a result of stress from prolonged lockdown orders, lost employment, and social isolation." Considering it was his behavior that prolonged the lockdown, this was hypocritical at best, and the most extreme form of gaslighting at worst.

The maliciously willful ineptitude undermined our faith in government. But Donald betrayed the people he lied to. Public denigration—started by him, echoed by his most vocal supporters, and amplified by right-wing media outlets—compromised the authority of his infectious disease experts, most notably Dr. Anthony Fauci, the longtime director of the National Institute of Allergy and Infectious Diseases, at the most critical time and led millions of American citizens to discount Fauci's expert advice about mask wearing and social distancing. To this day Donald has made a heroic vaccination campaign all the more difficult by sowing seeds of doubt about the very thing that can make this pandemic stop once and for all.

It was easy to be angry at people who refused to wear masks, but they were doing what many Americans have had ingrained in them from childhood—they were listening to their elected officials. They were listening to the people in whom they had put their trust with their votes— their mayor, their representative, their senator, their governor, or the man in the Oval Office. They can't be faulted for that. If you're a conservative in America, and your leaders are telling you that wearing a mask makes you a liberal, or makes you look weak, then you're going to show you're tough by refusing to wear one even if that means exposing you and those you love to a potentially deadly virus.

Like so much of government, the Centers for Disease Control and Prevention (CDC), which falls under the Department of Health and Human Services, has historically been allowed to do its work independently of politics. This changed after Michael Caputo, who had no previous experience in public health, was put in place to oversee the health department's communications. He in turn hired Paul Alexander, a part-time health professor, to an unpaid position as his science adviser. In May 2020, political appointees began to put pressure on the CDC when it released a report stating that community-wide mitigation efforts were needed to slow transmission. Eventually Robert Redfield, a virologist and director of the CDC, caved, allowed a political agenda to take precedence over science-based recommendations meant to protect the health and safety of the American people. Standard practice had been for hospitals to pass patient data and other relevant statistics to the CDC, which then compiled a database that was made publicly available. Without warning, hospitals were ordered instead to send data directly to HHS in Washington, where access by researchers and health officials who relied on the data for their decision-making processes was denied. Nothing like this had happened since the CDC's founding in 1946.

The COVID Tracking Project (CTP) was launched by *The Atlantic* in order to make up for this potentially devastating shift in policy. As journalist and founder of *Talking Points Memo* Josh Marshall wrote, "The project . . . was perhaps the most important single journalistic effort of the COVID pandemic, truly a marvel of synthesis, data visualization and fact-checking. And yet it was a genuine disgrace that it had to exist at all. This kind of effort is an elementary governmental and public health function. But the CDC just didn't do it."

By September, Paul Alexander was bragging about pressuring CDC officials to change their reports in order to reflect the administration's political message, not the science, all so they aligned with Donald's talking points.

How does an organization that should be entirely apolitical and left in the hands of people with the most expertise and the best chance of solving the problem get sidelined, its experts fired, in the process thwarting the actions that could be taken to save people?

How does one person have that much control over the CDC or the Defense Production Act or which states get vaccines or PPE? How is that allowed? Caputo was not a scientist, not a medical professional, not an epidemiologist. Yet, every step of the way, he interfered and did exactly the wrong thing even though he had at his disposal all of the necessary scientific expertise. He even accused the CDC of harboring a "resistance unit" opposed to Donald.

Other public servants were harassed, threatened, and forced to resign just when we needed them most.

A generation ago, the terrorist attacks of September 11, 2001, created a moment of great unity—not just in this country but across the world. We were all traumatized to varying degrees, and our shared horror created solidarity. We received the message that we were all in it together, no matter how far away from the attacks we were.

In January 2021, more people died nearly every day than were killed in the World Trade Center, yet COVID has been one of the most divisive tragedies in American history—all because one man didn't have the decency to wear a mask.

COVID is directly affecting every single person on the planet, creating an even greater opportunity to unite us around this common cause. Imagine if Donald's administration had led a global response to COVID. Imagine if we had helped other countries—that could have been unifying, too. A real leader would have said, "I don't care about politics or my reelection. My only mission is to do everything in my power to save lives." But Donald and his henchmen couldn't even see their way clear to getting help to states whose governors didn't kiss Donald's ass sufficiently.

After his release from Walter Reed Hospital, where he had been admitted after experiencing severe COVID symptoms, Donald climbed a grand exterior staircase to the White House's Truman balcony. Doing his best Mussolini imitation, he took off his mask in a macho display of invulnerability. He clenched his teeth and jutted out his jaw, just as my grandmother did when she was biting back anger or clamping down on her pain. In Donald, I saw the latter. I have asthma, so I am acutely aware of what it looks like when somebody is struggling to breathe. He was in pain, he was afraid, but he would never admit that to anybody—not even himself. Because, as always, the consequences of admitting vulnerability were much more frightening to him than being honest.

At the presidential debate in late September, shortly before his testing positive for COVID, he had mocked Joe Biden for wearing a mask at all times. Such mockery was wildly irresponsible, counterproductive, and dangerous in terms of public health.

In the more than two months between the election and Joe Biden's inauguration, Donald would go largely silent about the pandemic, aside from a handful of tweets mostly taking credit for Operation Warp Speed and Pfizer's development of a vaccine (which wasn't funded by Operation Warp Speed, although the federal government did commit to buying 100 million doses).

Donald's decisive loss meant the end of the federal government's conversation about COVID for the months he remained in office. There were no guidelines, no information, no leadership, no progress, and no more presidential briefings (although since they had often been fact-free and dangerous, this wasn't a bad thing). But Donald was still in the Oval Office and this country continued to suffer a mass casualty event every single day. Also, he had seventy-five more days to do a lot of damage.

He made the pivot to the Big Lie in the early morning hours after Election Day, before the results were even announced. He completely believed that he could turn things around. There was no reason for him not to—he always had. And let's face it, seventy-four million of us, if the 2020 election results are any indication, never felt that they'd been betrayed at all. Or, worse, those voters put the betrayal to the side because they understood the degree to which having a white supremacist in the Oval Office benefited them.

When your motive is not simply winning at all costs but grievance and revenge, you're more dangerous than a straight-up sociopath. Donald is much worse than that—he's someone with a gaping wound where his soul should be.

In one of his last tweets before he was removed from Twitter altogether, Donald slammed the CDC—his CDC—for exaggerating the case count and death toll. His denials notwithstanding, January 2021 would be the deadliest month in the United States since the virus began to spread a year earlier, killing one American every twenty-eight seconds.

PART III

American Exceptionalism

CHAPTER 5

Suffering in Silence

I t is a truism that the winners write history, and at the heart of our American system of government are an unacknowledged paradox and a false paradigm. The paradox is the unresolvable tension between the concepts of liberty and equality laid out in the Declaration of Independence and the embrace of chattel slavery in the Constitution. The paradigm is the myth that there is, first, such a thing as "race," and, second, that there is a fixed hierarchy with whites at the top and Blacks at the bottom.

Because of this paradox and false paradigm, the country has developed along two tracks that run parallel to each other but nevertheless continuously impact each other. One, based in historical fact, is the genocide of two groups of people—Native Americans and Africans—and the enslavement of the latter. The other is the myth of white supremacy, which is the story white America has told since the country's inception and that continues to drive the racial divide. It is the *denial* of white supremacy and the vehement need to deny it, however, that have ensured that the traumas upon which this country was founded would never heal, that they would in fact worsen over time, compounded by the continuing neglect of our democratic ideals and the pressing need of the white majority to pretend the traumas never happened.

Born in the flight from persecution and toward promise, our country was actually built on the backs and with the blood of Native Americans and enslaved Africans. When the Civil War ended, white Americans had a chance to atone, at least in some measure, by ensuring true equality for all people—by returning stolen land and sovereignty to Native Americans and guaranteeing and protecting freedmen and freedwomen's full rights as citizens.

The terrible irony is that white supremacy demanded that Blacks be excluded from society, despite their desire to be fully integrated, while Native Americans, who wanted nothing more than the return of their land and their sovereignty, were forced to assimilate, no matter what the cost to them.

We can only imagine, but never know, the trauma caused not only by the physical pain, but by the pain of isolation and despair and, once forced into the hostile world of the slave trader and the plantation, by the loss of dignity.

It's important to remember that although many Northerners hated slavery, they held deeply racist ideas about Black people. After all, running alongside the two and a half centuries of slavery were two and a half centuries' worth of *justifications* for slavery. Whether people owned other human beings or not, they all grew up in a society that both approved of slavery, and also, for the most part, espoused the beliefs that Black people are inferior and that

Christian doctrine supports their enslavement. If you lived in the North, slavery was unacceptable, but so too was the full equality of Black people.

Black achievement during Reconstruction was extraordinary. As social psychologist Susan Opotow writes, however, "Local inclusionary gains too may be lost if the larger society does not recognize, accept, and adopt them. There are more ways to achieve partial rather than complete inclusion. And there are more ways to fail than to succeed. For inclusionary efforts to influence the future of post-war societies, they need to be significant and sustained."

The scope of the postwar project was beyond the comprehension even of those who most supported Black suffrage and equality. In twelve short years Blacks were expected to prove their worth, despite having received no restitution and minimal assistance and, most consequentially, while living in a society that actively interfered with any attempts on the part of Blacks to exercise their newly won rights. What was *required* was for white attitudes about Blacks, which were the direct result of by now deeply ingrained and often unacknowledged racism and white supremacy, to be completely reversed. Under these circumstances failure was the only option. And by the end of Reconstruction, most Black Americans in the South had been effectively reenslaved. As Bryan Stevenson has said, "Slavery didn't end in 1865, it just evolved."

During the Jim Crow period, Black Americans continued to lose what they'd worked and suffered for. Pressure on Blacks to conform to rules imposed by the Redeemers increased, as did efforts to contain them. Black people who had achieved some measure of autonomy and sense of agency at the beginning of Reconstruction suddenly found themselves once again having to watch every move they made. Fear of doing the "wrong thing" pervaded the lives of Blacks and ground down any sense of safety or security, because in the end the "wrong thing" was Black existence. One tactic whites used in achieving this atmosphere of excessive caution was to inject uncertainty into even the most mundane encounters between whites and Blacks. Blacks could be arrested or lynched for such infractions as looking at a white woman the "wrong way," for not stepping off the sidewalk to make room for a white person, or for failing to call a white man "sir."

From the beginning, the goal for whites was the control not just of Black bodies but of Black agency. There is no way for a human being to live freely if the act of living itself is deemed dangerous and threatening by those in power. Otherwise, what conclusion can be drawn when the punishments were so incommensurate with the infractions? If Southern whites really believed that Blacks were incapable of feeling pain, then why did they go to such great lengths to cause them such agony? If you were a white man who believed so profoundly in your own native superiority, why did you need a mob of other white men to emasculate a Black man who'd already been rendered powerless? The backlash that accompanied each cycle of advancement was too strong to overcome. The urgency of white supremacy requires that white society always find a way to achieve homeostasis. In America this homeostasis can only occur when white people are at the top of the hierarchy and Black people are at the bottom of it.

In order to understand, as far as that's possible, the impact of the sustained trauma from the first generation of enslaved Africans onward, we need to put it in context.

One potential response when a person witnesses or experiences a traumatic event is for him or her to develop post-traumatic stress disorder. Symptoms may include intrusive memories, avoidance, alterations in moods and cognition, and changes in arousal. If untreated, these symptoms can persist over the course of a lifetime and significantly impact a person's ability to function.

The diagnosis of complex PTSD is a potential consequence if an individual is repeatedly subjected to a trauma or "totalitarian control over a prolonged period," according to Judith Herman, in her seminal work, *Trauma and Recovery*. Dr. Joy DeGruy, a researcher and educator, has introduced the concept of post-traumatic slave syndrome, "a condition that exists when a population has experienced multigenerational trauma resulting from centuries of slavery and continues to experience oppression and institutionalized racism today."

In addition to the traumatic fear of death enslaved people experienced every day of their lives, they were also subjected to spiritual abuse suffered when they lost their culture and were forbidden to practice their native religions; emotional abuse when forced to watch or participate in the abuse of other enslaved people or when separated from their families; psychological abuse resulting from the interdiction against literacy; sexual abuse in the form of rape or being forced to participate publicly in sexual acts; and physical abuse that took the form of whippings, beatings, and whatever creative tortures their "owners" could devise. The psychological and emotional impact of the totality of all of these abuses would have been incalculable. What would the effects be on the next generation and the generations to follow?

The field of epigenetics suggests that trauma can so profoundly affect our bodies that genetic markers are "placed" on our DNA. In this way the effects of trauma we experience can be passed on to subsequent generations, creating, according to Rachel Yehuda, a professor of psychiatry with a specialty in epigenetics, a "predisposition rather than an inevitable outcome." They can also increase both an individual's vulnerability and resilience. Either way, as she puts it, our traumatic "experiences lodge physiologically" and the effects of trauma endure.

Since the end of the Civil War the thing most likely to incite white violence against Black people was the success of Black people. Giving Blacks full rights beyond the freedom that had grudgingly been granted them proved to be a bridge too far for many whites, and any steps Blacks took to avail themselves of those rights triggered swift and severe reprisals. It seems self-evident that the driver behind the essential reenslavement of Black people was Black prosperity.

The establishment of Black communities united by churches and benevolent societies, schools, and, most significantly, political organizations that resulted in real electoral power threatened the Southern ideal of white supremacy. And while Blacks understood the power of achieving literacy, whites understood the threat that literacy posed. Disrupting the spread of knowledge among the Black community became an important tactic in the project to reestablish and maintain the antebellum white social order in the postwar South. Because literacy rates were so low, educated Blacks often served in more than one leadership role. As Susan Opotow writes, "Violence by terrorist groups limited the ability of the black community to sustain an influential presence in Southern decision-making institutions, destroying a political and social movement by targeting the intelligentsia." This strategy was called sophiacide, literally, the "killing of knowledge."

Black prosperity was punished with relentless savagery. When Black soldiers returned home after World War I and World War II wearing their uniforms, proud to have served their country with honor, they were treated like a threat to the established racial hierarchy, because they were. While Black veterans expected that their having served would confer on them a certain respect, white people interpreted their expectation as arrogance. That a Black man would think himself equal to a white man could not be allowed to stand; Black veterans were beaten and lynched, their uniforms a visible reminder of their equality and an implicit rebuke to the white man's false sense of superiority.

Black Americans had to try ten times as hard to achieve one-tenth as much, and Black people's success even in the face of the obstacles placed before them was the greatest offense against white supremacy. It was also the most dangerous challenge to it. Mostly through violence but also through legislative means, whites impeded, undermined, and reversed Black advancement with complete impunity. Law enforcement was often involved or looked the other way.

The 1921 massacre in Tulsa, Oklahoma, which has been called the nadir of race relations in this country, was a direct result of the white supremacist hatred of Black success. Fifteen years after it had been established by O. W. Gurley, a wealthy Black American from Alabama, Greenwood was a thriving, predominantly Black section of Tulsa with over ten thousand residents, dubbed "Negro Wall Street" by Booker T. Washington because of its successful businesses and affluent inhabitants. As Greenwood became more prosperous and populous, however, tensions with the neighboring white population simmered.

On May 31, 1921, white citizens finally found a reason to retaliate when Dick Rowland, a nineteen-year-old Black man, entered an elevator in a downtown building operated by a seventeen-year-old white girl named Sarah Page. We don't know specifically what happened between them, but shortly after Rowland entered the elevator Page screamed. Knowing what assumptions might be made and what danger they would put him in, Rowland fled. When questioned by police, Page stated that Rowland did grab her arm, but she did not consider it an assault and she declined to press charges. Word that Rowland had indeed assaulted Page, however, got out into the larger white community and a manhunt ensued.

Rowland was arrested the next day and, due to a threat on his life, taken to a secure jail at the county courthouse. In short order a white mob formed outside. Black residents from Greenwood feared the worst, and approximately fifty men armed themselves and proceeded to the courthouse in the hope that they could keep Rowland safe. By the time they arrived, the crowd of white men had swelled to over a thousand. An altercation broke out when a white man attempted to take a Black man's gun. The weapon accidentally discharged and all hell broke loose. Within minutes several Black men were lying dead in the street.

At dawn the next day, as many as fifteen hundred National Guardsmen, police officers, and the white mob, many of its members having been deputized by the police, streamed through Greenwood, looting and burning businesses and homes. By the time it was over, three hundred Black people had been murdered, some of them shot in the back or burned to death, and the neighborhood had been razed.

Blacks who survived were placed in internment camps. Thirty-five square blocks had been destroyed and the equivalent of thirty-two million dollars lost. When the smoke cleared it was as if Greenwood had never existed. For decades, history failed to record that the massacre itself had happened. Newspaper accounts were never transferred to microfilm. Books made no mention of it. Even eyewitnesses kept silent—white participants out of shame, and Black victims out of a desire to spare their children the fear and pain they had experienced.

This was not the first or the last racially motivated mass murder in this country: Black men, women, and children were murdered frequently, usually without consequence to the murderers. In fact, there were thirty-four documented massacres during Reconstruction alone and at least twelve between 1908 and 1923, with four in 1919. But what happened in Tulsa was emblematic of the intense racial animosity felt by whites and the backlash Blacks could expect for having the audacity to thrive.

On either side of the divide, we carry these holocausts with us in the present and into the future, whether as a victim or—either through identification or benefit—the guilty.

The assault on rights was inexorable, the terror and violence unceasing, and the value of what was stolen beyond measure, yet white America still refuses to acknowledge the harm done even to the perpetrators, let alone the victims. By that I don't mean to excuse or absolve their behavior or in any way equate the suffering of the two groups. Rather, it's important to highlight the necessity of identifying what went wrong on the individual, intrapersonal, interpersonal, and societal levels that caused people to behave so monstrously and feel justified in doing so to the extent that they kept letting themselves and each other off the hook.

In many of these cases, but by no means all of them, we know the names of the victims, but the perpetrators, the ordinary men who committed these barbaric crimes, and the white women who enabled them, suffered no consequences and instead, proud of what they had done or participated in or witnessed, went home to their families and lived out their lives without legal consequence. Sometimes the wives of these men accompanied them to the lynchings, complicit in their crimes, and sometimes their children came, too, witnesses to monstrosities against other human beings committed in the name of whiteness, which they were taught to celebrate. In photographs, whether of lynchings or of scenes of forced school integration, I look at the faces of the white children. Some seem confused. Sometimes their faces are brightened by smiles or contorted with rage and loathing. Not infrequently they look afraid. How many of these children grew up to espouse their parents' white supremacy, as James Eastland did? How many, traumatized by violence and the glorification of it, grew up permanently damaged?

CHAPTER 6

We Hold These Truths

D espite the centuries-long project to prove otherwise, and as much as many of us still believe otherwise, there is no truth to the myth of white superiority. That fact, unfortunately, is irrelevant in the context of the power inherent in the racial hierarchy white people have built. White supremacy is an increasingly powerful construct that spins a narrative designed to confer power on whites and deny it to Blacks. It teaches whites across generations that their race confers upon them significant advantage and prestige. The theories upon which these beliefs are based are utter nonsense. The advantages, however, are quite real.

Given that white supremacy seemingly runs through every strand of fabric from which this country has been woven, it's understandable that one might conclude that it is a uniquely American phenomenon. It was brought to the Northeast coast by the Puritans, however, along with their stringent brand of Reformation Protestantism known as Calvinism. In search of freedom to worship, for themselves if not for anyone else, the original settlers of what would eventually be called New England embraced concepts of whiteness, white superiority, and Protestantism as fiercely as they embraced Calvin's theology.

While the Reformation in general represented a turning away from the Renaissance and the Enlightenment and all the advances in science, intellectual exploration, and art they represented—anything that was not aligned with biblical teachings—John Calvin's insistence upon the totality of this rejection and the righteousness of his own cause bordered on, or crossed into, the fanatical. (He once claimed that proponents of the heliocentric model of the universe exhibited "monstrousness" and that "the devil possesses them," simply because they thought the Earth moved through space—which it does.)

Calvin's doctrine of predestination posited that only a select few have been chosen by God for salvation, and everybody else, regardless of the quality of the mortal lives they lead, is condemned to eternal damnation. The belief that good works have no impact on the disposition of one's soul might have influenced the development of the character of the future American. It also might explain, at least in part, the enduring myth of rugged individualism that continues to plague us. When people searched for clues to their divine fate, the conclusion was drawn (probably by people of means) that material wealth was the most obvious sign of God's mercy. Not much about this assumption had changed by the time Fred Trump began to espouse Norman Vincent Peale's "The Power of Positive Thinking" in the 1950s, and not much has changed since then.

By contrast, poverty marked you out as one of the damned. It was through this lens that slavery came to be seen as a self-fulfilling prophecy of Black inferiority. Enslavement was the destiny of the enslaved and the clearest sign that Blacks were not deserving of God's grace. In this way slavery and the genocide of Native Americans could both be accepted and, as a result, Black labor could be believed to have no value, existing only as something to be taken with impunity by their white "owners."

When European explorers first touched down on these shores, there were as many as six hundred distinct tribes with advanced cultures and languages comprising approximately seven million people. The Europeans' drive to conquer the land and spread their faith made them pitiless. The Puritans looked upon Native Americans as barbarians and savages to justify their wholesale slaughter. They were infidels against whom a holy war must be fought. And so it was, unceasingly, for decades. Only 225,000 survived into the twentieth century.

In *Representing Whiteness in the Black Imagination*, bell hooks neatly describes how "Black folks associated whiteness with the terrible, the terrifying, and the terrorizing." This is an apt distillation of the way whites have structured society in order to prop up white supremacy. The myth of supremacy is an exercise in projection, which continues to be a powerful tool for whites in power and gestures at the reality that has been grounded in their perpetuation of a cycle of fear, control, and violence throughout generations.

For example, white people fear Blacks and the loss of power they would suffer if Blacks gained their autonomy. These fears created the need for control and the necessity of forming groups that can exercise that control. Under certain circumstances, control leads to violence and terrorism—for example, lynchings and KKK cross burnings. And when Blacks seek to protect themselves—as they did in numerous slave rebellions, during the Tulsa massacre, and in civil rights protests from the 1960s through today—whites then claim it is Blacks who are violent, which kicks the cycle off again.

Two things needed to happen in order for the colonists to rid the land of the natives and maintain an enormous population of enslaved Africans. First, both groups had to be "racialized." Although hundreds of distinct native communities may have existed when the settlers first arrived, they were all placed into one racial category—Indian. The Africans, too, had come from diverse tribes and rich cultures, but they were distilled into the homogenous unit called Black.

Second, both of these daunting tasks demanded white unity. In order for this to be accomplished, wealthy white landowners had to make common cause with white indentured servants and poor laborers who actually had more to gain, from an economic perspective, by joining with Blacks. This potential alliance would endanger both the landowners' wealth and the racial hierarchy, as white laborers in the South comprised 60 percent of the white population (while Blacks comprised 20 percent of the total population).

The historian Philip Rubio believes that unity across class lines was achieved because white laborers were bribed—whether through the promise of free land after the term of their servitude had expired or a reduction in poll taxes—by wealthy landowners. Either way, the overarching effect was the strengthening of white racial identity. Going forward, the white working class would remain committed to the cause of white power and privilege, from which they would continue to benefit. Over the centuries, more ways would be found to strengthen this commitment.

From the beginning, the colonists, and then white Americans, were united in their goal to keep enslaved Blacks under control. And white identity played an increasing role in American society and institutions.

The drive to purify the nation's racial makeup continued with the Naturalization Act of 1790, which restricted immigration and naturalization to "free white persons." It wasn't until the Immigration and Nationality Act of 1965 was passed, 175 years later, that race, religion, and nationality were eliminated as bases for admission to the United States. Only when the Trump administration's Muslim ban was signed by executive order in January 2017 was an interdiction once again placed on the immigration of nonwhites and non-Christians.

While definitions of whiteness—or rather of who could be white—became more flexible throughout the twentieth century, being Black continued to remain a barrier to entry into white society and Black Americans continued to be barred from opportunities for prosperity.

After rioting during the Depression led to the legalization of unions, no anti-discrimination amendment was attached to the legislation because the AFL and CIO opposed it. For decades, whites would have job security as well as access to union-only jobs, and Blacks would have neither.

Although people don't typically think of the G.I. Bill this way, Rubio describes it as "legislation that enhanced white supremacy." While it provided government jobs, low-interest mortgages, and free college educations to white men who had served in the military during World War II, Black veterans were left out. The extent to which this widened even further the gap between white and Black wealth—in terms of education, real property and savings, and the success of future generations—is likely immeasureable.

"If the white race was invented in colonial America," Rubio writes, "one could argue that it was reinvented with the post–World War Two suburbs."

• • •

The breadth and depth of Protestantism's influence on American culture and politics gives the lie to the idea that America is "neutral in religious matters," the First Amendment notwithstanding. Freedom of religion has typically meant freedom to practice Protestantism.

Puritans remained convinced past reason that their view was not just the right view but the only view. Any beliefs that deviated from theirs weren't simply apostasy, they were ridiculous and not to be credited. Over time, the tenets of white supremacy and the Puritan worldview would become inextricably intertwined. And we've seen how dedicated this country has been to maintaining both.

The idea that America could be seen as God's chosen land, providentially ordained to lead a world that would otherwise lapse into barbarism, carried with it an apocalyptic cast that would frame other battles. World War II and the Cold War were couched in terms of "good" and "evil." Ronald Reagan's 1983 reference to the Soviet Union as the "evil empire" and "the focus of evil in the modern world" implied that America was on the side of good in that fight—and that God was on our side.

Since at least the nineteenth century, biological determinism—the idea that all science is objective (it is not) and that differences between groups are inherited—has been the basis for some of the most influential and self-serving theories about racial differences. From craniometry—the "science" of measuring skulls—to IQ testing, racist, pseudoscientific arguments have been used to measure white superiority and establish the inferiority of pretty much everybody else.

Social Darwinism was the inane theory that attempted to co-opt Darwin's theory of evolution in an effort to demonstrate that the racial and social hierarchies were determined by the survival of the fittest.

Very popular in America, social Darwinism was also used to justify the atrocities of genocide and slavery. Poverty and failure to succeed were seen as proof that those at the bottom deserved to be there. Wealth, on the other hand, was seen as an indicator of innate superiority, which explains why magnates like John D. Rockefeller and Andrew Carnegie subscribed wholeheartedly to the theory.

The project of scientific racism became more sophisticated with the development of the intelligence quotient, or IQ, test. Originally designed by Frenchman Alfred Binet in 1904 to help evaluate children with special learning needs, the test itself was not inherently racist. Binet understood that children develop at varying rates, and that human intelligence is diverse and irreducible (not able to be reduced to one monolithic measurement).

But recognizing the potential for Binet's test to prove "scientifically" the superiority of the white race, H. H. Goddard, a leading eugenicist at the time, introduced it to America. Goddard's goal was completely contrary to Binet's intentions. The extent to which IQ is heritable isn't known, but we do know that it cannot be reduced to a single number. Yet that is what American IQ tests, which were relied upon throughout much of the twentieth century, set out to do. The tests were also heavily biased toward white culture and white experience while making no allowances for differences in environmental and other factors like socioeconomic status, education, family background, language proficiency, nutrition, or health. What people like Goddard and Carl Brigham, who developed the SAT, failed (or refused) to realize was that whether intelligence is largely heritable or not, it is malleable. Brigham was so convinced otherwise that he believed IQ tests "had proven beyond any scientific doubt that, like the American Negroes, the Italians and the Jews were genetically ineducable. It would be a waste of good money even to attempt to try to give these born morons and imbeciles a good Anglo-Saxon education."

The tests, which were neither reliable nor valid, had merely fulfilled the expectations of their designers—that whites were intellectually superior to all other races and belonged squarely at the top of the hierarchy and Blacks, intellectually limited and uneducable, were at the bottom.

Many American proponents of IQ testing also, not coincidentally, were staunch eugenicists—they believed in the practice of selective breeding of people in the superior races (upper-class white women were often refused birth control for this reason) and the targeted sterilization of those in undesirable groups, which in early twentieth-century America meant the poor, the disabled, the intellectually limited (or, to use the technical terms of the day, "morons," "idiots," and "imbeciles"), immigrants, and of course Blacks.

While English eugenics focused on breeding for positive traits, American eugenics—whose proponents included Alexander Graham Bell and President Woodrow Wilson—was more focused on removing negative traits by, essentially, removing undesirables. More than thirty states enacted sterilization laws after the turn of the twentieth century. In an infamous 1927 case, *Buck v. Bell*, the Supreme Court legitimized the movement even further when it ruled that the state of Virginia had the right to sterilize a young white woman named Carrie Buck, who had given birth out of wedlock at the age of seventeen. Carrie later claimed the pregnancy was the result of her having been raped by her foster mother's nephew. The court, however, seemed interested only in the argument made by an expert witness, who had never met Buck, that, having led a life of promiscuity and immorality, she belonged to "the shiftless, ignorant, and worthless class of anti-social whites of the South."

The court ruled against Buck. In his opinion, Justice Oliver Wendell Holmes Jr. wrote, "It is better for all the world, if instead of waiting to execute degenerate offspring for crime, or to let them starve for imbecility, society can prevent those who are manifestly unfit from continuing their kind. . . . Three generations of imbeciles is enough."

It's shocking, but not surprising, that Holmes's reputation as a tireless supporter of civil rights survived this opinion. It's not shocking that eugenics programs flourished after this ruling, emerging, as journalist Andrea DenHoed writes in a 2016 *New Yorker* article, "The Forgotten Lessons of the American Eugenics Movement," "where the variously unfit could be committed for a short time, sterilized, and then released, like cats, back into the general population, with the happy assurance that they would never reproduce."

The American eugenics movement was influential throughout the world in the years before World War II. Hitler specifically made reference to California's eugenics program—between 1909 and 1979, at least twenty thousand people were forcibly sterilized under its auspices. The American South, with its extensive and comprehensive laws governing segregation, miscegenation, and the project to keep Blacks in the role of second-class citizens, led the world in race-based legislation.

For Nazis, with their own ambitious goals for racial purity, the accomplishments of the American South in this regard were the gold standard. When German lawyers met in 1934 to draft legislation that would become the basis for the Nuremberg Laws, the South's total success in depriving Blacks of their rights was a major topic of conversation.

By the time the Constitution was written, white supremacy was already woven into the DNA of the British colonies and their white inhabitants. Despite the soaring rhetoric Thomas Jefferson used to write the Declaration of Independence, he believed whites were intellectually superior to Blacks, and his judgment had an outsized influence.

The conditions of white supremacy were codified in the Constitution, as was the notion, enshrined in the appalling "three-fifths compromise," that Blacks were not fully human, crafted by James Madison as a way to bring pro- and anti-abolition factions together. Blacks would be counted as three-fifths of a person for the purposes of determining population as well as for the purposes of taxation. This gave the South extra representation in the House of Representatives, which in itself would have long-term consequences, while giving the enslaved no say at all in how they were governed.

The English abolitionist Thomas Day noted the hypocrisy when he wrote in 1776, "If there be an object truly ridiculous in nature, it is an American patriot, signing resolutions of independency with the one hand, and with the other brandishing a whip over his affrighted slaves."

The devastating and far-reaching impact this decision would have on the future of the country and its hundreds of thousands of enslaved people can't be overestimated; and considering that the words "white," "Black," "slave," and "slavery" do not appear anywhere in the Constitution, the founders, or at least some of them, were not entirely sanguine about it. The amendments righting this wrong were more than eighty years in the future (the founders, of course, would have no idea how many decades or centuries into the future slavery would continue to exist), condemning four more generations of Blacks to a brutal life of bondage.

This failure of humanity didn't occur because a majority of the colonies insisted upon keeping slavery legal. Quite the opposite. Only South Carolina and Georgia refused to give in on their insistence that they be allowed to keep the people they'd enslaved. The real obstacle was the so-called liberals of the North who wanted slavery abolished but wished to maintain their political power. Unable to resolve this contradiction, they deferred to the slave states.

In order to make the Constitution democratic, the Supreme Court and Congress would have to do some heavy lifting. Since SCOTUS is the final arbiter of what laws will or will not stand, however, it is worth looking at how this revered body has responded historically to America's evolution and the role it has played in helping America fulfill its great potential.

The verdict is not good. Although it may sound counterintuitive, in the nearly two and a half centuries of its existence, the Supreme Court has been one of the most antidemocratic forces in our history.

The details of how the court would function and who would be able to serve on it were not spelled out in the Constitution. The Judiciary Act of 1789 determined that there would be six justices on the Supreme Court, but beyond that the president and Congress would have to work out the specifics. Until 1869, the number of justices on the court fluctuated between five and ten, sometimes to accommodate a growing population and territory, but mostly for political reasons.

After Andrew Johnson vetoed the Civil Rights Act of 1866, the Republican Congress, concerned that the president would install justices sympathetic to the South, reduced the size of the court to seven. Once the Republican Ulysses Grant came into office in 1869, two more seats were added. The number of justices has remained nine ever since.

And over and over again the nine have handed down decisions that, were it not for the ineluctable influence of white supremacy, made no sense in the context of a constitutional democratic republic.

The string of antidemocratic decisions started before the Civil War, with the court's ruling in the 1857 *Dred Scott* case. Scott, who had been born into slavery, had been brought to Illinois, a free state, by his enslaver. When they returned to Missouri, a slave state, Scott sued for his freedom, claiming that he had been free in Illinois and should be allowed to remain free. When state and federal courts ruled against him, he appealed to the Supreme Court. The opinion, written by Chief Justice Roger Taney, concluded that "[Black people] are not included, and were not intended to be included, under the word 'citizens' in the Constitution, and can therefore claim none of the rights and privileges which that instrument provides for." He went even further, claiming that individual states could not grant Blacks state citizenship, because "[the negro] had no rights which the white man was bound to respect; and that the negro might justly and lawfully be reduced to slavery for his benefit."

Unbelievably, Taney and the other six justices who sided with him thought that their decision would definitively settle the question of slavery and calm the tensions that had been growing between North and South for years. This couldn't have been further from the truth, and the *Scott* decision brought the nation several steps closer to civil war.

We've learned over the last two and a half centuries that, although rights can be granted by Congress, the Supreme Court doesn't necessarily guarantee them. In the decades following the Civil War, the court demonstrated this most glaringly in several decisions that severely compromised the seminal advances achieved during Reconstruction with the passage of the Thirteenth, Fourteenth, and Fifteenth Amendments. In the years 1865 to 1878, in fact, the Supreme Court embarked on one of the greatest assaults on democracy in the history of this country.

From the nation's founding until 1865, the Supreme Court had struck down just two congressional acts as unconstitutional. Between 1865 and 1876, the court did so thirteen times, including its decision on the Enforcement Acts of 1871 (of which the Ku Klux Klan Act was the third), which came five years later in *United States v. Cruikshank*.

The case arose after as many as 280 Blacks were massacred, some after having surrendered, in the aftermath of a gubernatorial election in Louisiana in which both sides had declared victory. Although some of the white perpetrators were indicted and set to face federal charges, as provided for by the Enforcement Act, when the case got to the Supreme Court, a majority ruled that the charges against individuals who were not state actors were unconstitutional because the federal charges infringed upon states' rights. In other words, the federal government had no power to prosecute individuals who committed terrorist acts *even if the state refused to do so*. The defendants' convictions were overturned, and the decision seriously undermined the equal-protection clause of the Fourteenth Amendment ("nor shall any State deprive any person of life, liberty, or property, without due process of law; nor deny to any person within its jurisdiction the equal protection of laws"), as well as the safety, suffrage, and freedom of Southern Blacks.

The court continued to strike blows against the Fourteenth Amendment when, in 1896, it issued its decision in *Plessy v. Ferguson*. The case had been brought by Homer Plessy, who had been charged with riding in a whites-only train car—even though he was seven-eighths white. The 7–1 majority opinion held that the Fourteenth Amendment "could not have been intended to abolish distinctions based upon color, or to enforce social, as distinguished from political equality, or a commingling of the two races upon terms unsatisfactory to either."

Only seven years later, the court heard *Giles v. Harris*, the case of Jackson Giles, a courageous Black man from Alabama who, after voting for thirty years, was prohibited from doing so in 1901 because of regressive changes to voting rights enshrined in the state's new constitution that disproportionately affected Black Americans. Giles claimed that the new laws violated his Fifteenth Amendment rights. The court doesn't seem to have addressed that question directly but instead ruled that, because the plaintiffs wanted to be registered to vote despite claiming the state's new voting restrictions were unconstitutional, registering them would not remedy the situation. So the plaintiffs were disenfranchised and the unconstitutional state law was left to stand.

In *The Color of Law,* Richard Rothstein points to two more recent cases involving desegregation, both of which underscore the court's tendency to ignore its own history and evidence that contradict its own preconceived notions.

In *Milliken v. Bradley,* a 1974 case about school segregation in Detroit public schools, the plaintiffs argued that, because neighborhoods had been racially segregated as the direct result of government policy, segregating schools was unconstitutional. Despite the fact that school segregation was indeed the *direct result* of decades of housing segregation mandated by local, state, and federal government agencies and that plaintiffs had presented evidence proving this, the court ruled against them. The majority opinion, written by Chief Justice Warren Burger, claimed that as long as school districts had no racist intent in drawing district lines, there was no obligation for them to desegregate. Ignoring evidence that had been presented to the court, Burger continued, "No record has been made in this case showing that the racial composition of the Detroit school population or that residential patterns within Detroit and in the surrounding areas were in any significant measure caused by governmental activity." This conclusion was absurd on its face.

In his dissent, Justice Thurgood Marshall wrote, "Our Nation, I fear, will be ill served by the Court's refusal to remedy separate and unequal education, for unless our children begin to learn together, there is little hope our people will ever learn to live together." His concerns proved prescient when after the ruling the schools and neighborhoods of Detroit became even more segregated.

Over thirty years later, Chief Justice John Roberts would join in a majority opinion that echoed Chief Justice Burger's, claiming that school districts in Louisville and Seattle could not use students' race as a metric in integration plans. Roberts wrote that segregated neighborhoods may be the result of "societal discrimination," but the discrimination itself was "not traceable to [government's] own actions."

"This misrepresentation of our racial history," Rothstein concludes, "indeed this willful blindness, became the consensus view of American jurisprudence."

Although President Biden's executive order calling for the formation of a bipartisan Presidential Commission on the Supreme Court has been characterized by the right as partisan, it's hard to argue against discussing potential reforms. As the White House statement about the order reads, the commission will examine "the Court's role in the Constitutional system; the length of service and turnover of justices on the Court; the membership and size of the Court; and the Court's case selection, rules, and practices."

In April 2021, Justice Stephen Breyer aired his thoughts on expanding the court with the intention of making "those whose initial instincts may favor important structural change or other similar institutional change, such as forms of court-packing, think long and hard before they embody those changes in law." Given the court's recent history, Breyer's concerns seem misguided at best. Structurally, the court would benefit from an overhaul, and there is nothing in the Constitution or the Judiciary Act that says it can't be done. Between lifetime appointments and the vagaries of chance, Barack Obama, who won the popular vote by 9.5 million votes in 2008 and five million in 2012 and served eight years in office, was able to appoint only two Supreme Court justices. Donald, who *lost* the popular vote to Hillary Clinton by almost three million votes and was in office for only four years (and impeached twice), was able to appoint three.

And, of course, then–Senate majority leader Mitch McConnell blocked President Obama from filling Justice Antonin Scalia's seat because "the American people should have a voice in the selection of their next Supreme Court Justice. Therefore, this vacancy should not be filled until we have a new president." Obama had eleven months remaining and yet his nominee, Merrick Garland, never received a hearing. Republican senators refused to meet with Garland even privately. Ruth Bader Ginsburg died *six weeks* before the next presidential election, yet Amy Coney Barrett was confirmed in thirty days. Currently, Breyer's newest colleague is refusing to recuse herself from the case of a litigant, Americans for Prosperity, which announced upon her nomination that it was funding a "Full Scale Campaign to Confirm Judge Amy Coney Barrett to the Supreme Court," with financing in the seven figures.

Every member of the federal judiciary is subject to a code of conduct—with a small number of exceptions, including Supreme Court justices. Believing even justices should be subject to an ethics code, Democrats have introduced legislation only to be met with resistance from Republicans. Chief Justice John Roberts also does not believe that Supreme Court members need to be bound by an ethics code. And yet Breyer is concerned that "if the public sees judges as politicians in robes, its confidence in the courts—and in the rule of law itself—can only diminish, diminishing the court's power, including its power to act as a check on other branches. . . . Structural alteration motivated by the perception of political influence can only feed that latter perception, further eroding that trust."

As First Amendment attorney Anne Champion wrote: "The Court has eroded trust in itself through politicized decisions from Dred Scott on down." The idea that attempting to reform a body that has done so much damage to democracy is somehow dangerous to its integrity would be laughable if it had been said by anybody other than a Supreme Court justice.

It's remarkable how often justices seem to be ignorant of the history of their own institution and blind to the behavior of their colleagues, but it has happened time and time again throughout our history; such ignorance and blindness among the justices appear to be part of the court's history as well.

In response to news of Biden's Commission on the Supreme Court, Aaron Belkin, the director of the group Take Back the Court, said, "There's growing recognition that the Supreme Court poses a danger to the health and well-being of the nation and even to democracy itself. A White House judicial reform commission has a historic opportunity to explain the gravity of the threat and to help contain it by urging Congress to add seats, which is the only way to restore balance to the court."

It is an especially bitter irony that the very institution created to rule objectively on legal matters related to our founding documents and principles has become so deeply partisan that it can no longer be regarded as worthy of our trust.

PART IV

The Reckoning

CHAPTER 7

The Precipice

This is democracy's day," President Joe Biden said in his inaugural address on January 20, 2021. "A day of history and hope. Of renewal and resolve. Through a crucible for the ages America has been tested anew and America has risen to the challenge. Today, we celebrate the triumph not of a candidate, but of a cause, the cause of democracy. The will of the people has been heard and the will of the people has been heeded. We have learned again that democracy is precious. Democracy is fragile. And at this hour, my friends, democracy has prevailed."

We needed those words, we needed that hope, and, it turns out, we needed the inauguration, *his* inauguration, to be held in front of the Capitol. I had worried that this gathering would be dangerous, given the horrific scene there just two weeks earlier and the continuing threat posed by those who refused to accept the election results, but Biden made the right choice—to stand where presidents before him have stood. It was important to have one less thing taken away from us, to be reminded that, when the will is there to protect our freedoms, they will be protected.

I'm not sanguine about how triumphantly democracy has prevailed, however. America dodged a bullet—figuratively, when Donald lost his bid for reelection, and literally, when his most ardent followers stormed the seat of government in a violent attempt to prevent the certification of Biden's definitive win. But, while it's true that we snatched democracy from the jaws of autocracy, there is still a gun pointed at democracy's head.

A democratic process, like an election, cannot fix the problems of a democracy if that process is deliberately hamstrung by a major political party that wants to do away with democracy in order to maintain its power in the face of a changing electorate whose interests the party only occasionally represents. And we're still staring down the barrel of a potential crisis resulting from a fragile economy, the ravages of COVID, and a looming mental health crisis after more than a year of isolation and dread. There is much talk about returning to normal, but our normal wasn't something to aspire to. As a country, as a society, there was, and is, much that remains broken. After this dual crisis of a government that nearly failed us and an existential threat to our very lives, we have an opportunity to make this country a better, more livable place for everyone, not just the privileged majority.

After the Civil War, the North had opportunities to right the wrongs committed during the colonial era and the first ninety years of this country's existence. The North could have made the South pay for the damage it had done to the nation by trying the leaders of the Confederacy as traitors. The North could have dedicated proper resources, including offering free land and community assistance in the form of schools and hospitals, so that freed Blacks were at least somewhat compensated for the centuries of stolen labor and would have had a fairer shot at acquiring financial freedom. With their financial and political power hobbled, the ability of white Southerners to engage in organized and legislatively sanctioned terroristic violence would have been curtailed.

After World War II, the New Deal and the benefits of the G.I. Bill could have been extended to Black Americans, allowing them to accumulate wealth and education to the same degree their white counterparts did.

At almost every step of the way in our history, there were opportunities to make this country more democratic, more open, and more equitable. Instead, the North became more segregated and the South continued to be a closed fascist state. The political will to do the right thing was lacking, and one could argue that a scaffolding upon which a fully democratic society could be sustained had not yet been built.

By the same token, between the 2020 election and the inauguration seventy-eight days later, the Republican Party and its leadership were presented with many off-ramps (as they had been as soon as Donald announced his candidacy in 2015) that would have prevented or at least mitigated the damage Donald, as lame duck, was able to cause. From Mitch McConnell on down, the party could have immediately accepted the results of the election on November 7 as soon as media outlets declared Joe Biden the president-elect and Kamala Harris the vice president–elect. They could have ignored Donald and countered or even condemned his Big Lie while pointing out that his concession was not required in order for the election results to be certified. His lie therefore, like him, would have been irrelevant.

The party could have taken strong positions against Donald's frivolous lawsuits. They could have condemned the conspiracies and the incitement leading up to the January 6 insurrection. And finally, they could have convicted Donald in the Senate after his second impeachment, or at least invoked the third section of the Fourteenth Amendment, which states, "No person shall be a Senator or Representative in Congress, or elector of President and Vice-President, or hold any office, civil or military, under the United States, or under any state, who, having previously taken an oath . . . to support the Constitution of the United States, shall have engaged in insurrection or rebellion against the same, or given aid or comfort to the enemies thereof." If nothing else, taking that step would have made it impossible for Donald to pretend he planned to run for the presidency again in 2024, and thereby shut down his ability to raise money off that pretense. But even that wouldn't have been much help. By failing to act immediately after media outlets announced Biden's victory, the party gave Donald more than two months to spread the Big Lie, gain adherents, and undermine the legitimacy and effectiveness of the incoming Biden administration. In the short term, the already anemic fight against COVID was weakened even further, placing untold millions of lives at greater risk. In the long run, the sanctity of our elections and, therefore, our entire system of government were put at risk.

People tend to shy away from language that seems extreme—as if it's rude or using it would make them seem melodramatic or unhinged. If we don't call things what they are, if we don't use language honestly, we can't expect people to understand what's really going on. By failing to use language accurately—because it would be impolite or we don't want to offend anybody—we set up a situation in which describing the Republican Party as a party of fascists leads people to question the extremity of the *language* rather than the validity of the premise.

But what else do you call it when a mob of white men shouts "Jews will not replace us" in the service of protecting a statue of Robert E. Lee? How else do you describe a party that didn't just tolerate but supported putting children in concentration camps; suppressing dissent during peaceful Black Lives Matter protests with seemingly unidentified para-militaries; dismantling truth and distrusting reality; designating a free press and whistleblowers as enemies of the people—and by extension of the state? How do you describe a party that made one of its chief goals the theocratization of the federal judiciary? If anybody thinks after all of this that calling them fascist is rude, then we have a very serious problem.

The real damage, however, was done by the Republican Party's fail-ure to hold Donald accountable after his first impeachment. Democrats in the House had laid out clear evidence that Donald was guilty of the crimes of abuse of power in attempting to coerce Volodymyr Zelensky into finding—or manufacturing—compromising information about Joe Biden in an effort to steal the election and obstruction of justice in refusing to submit requested documents to the Judiciary Committee, ignoring subpoenas, and blocking the testimony of anybody in his ad-ministration. In spite of this, or more likely because of it, then–majority leader Mitch McConnell refused to allow Democrats to call witnesses during the Senate trial.

The failure to remove him from office allowed Donald to run for reelection with yet another grievance with which to stir up his already aggrieved base. While the proceedings were still ongoing, he had tweeted, "SUCH ATROCIOUS LIES BY THE RADICAL LEFT, DO NOTHING DEMOCRATS. THIS IS AN ASSAULT ON AMER-ICA, AND AN ASSAULT ON THE REPUBLICAN PARTY!!!!"

Worst of all, though, was the fact that seventy-four million people had the chance to express support for him with their votes, thereby emboldening him, empowering each other, and amplifying their ideology.

The Republicans had believed from the beginning that they could harness Donald's hold on the base and use it to their own advantage while controlling him. Because of Donald's willingness to go along with any policy they proposed, and to break promises and shatter norms, congressional Republicans had a two-year stretch of almost unimpeded success—if you measure success by the number of judges confirmed and the amount of money gifted to the richest individuals and corporations in the form of tax cuts.

In the end, it looked like they had made a bad bargain.

In the early hours of November 4, 2020, with seven states still too close to call and three days before the results of the election would be definitively known, Donald claimed victory. He called for "all voting to stop" because continuing to count ballots would be to commit a "fraud on the American people." Just as Attorney General Bill Barr had done before the release of the Mueller report, creating a false narrative with the intention of shaping reactions, Donald was planting the seeds of doubt and grievance as, for the first time in modern American history, the loser refused to concede a presidential election.

The real premise of the Big Lie was that a majority of voters that included a diverse coalition of liberals, progressives, people of color, and LGBTQ people wasn't *really* a majority at all. More pointedly, the message was a continuation of a message that had been sent to Black Americans since Reconstruction—your votes don't count.

The claims of voter fraud were brazen enough, considering that the 2020 election was determined to be the most secure in American history by Donald's own Department of Homeland Security. In the context of the extraordinary amount of Republican-backed voter suppression that occurred in many red states around the country, the claims amounted to more gaslighting.

The Big Lie gave Republican state legislatures and attorneys general a pretense for ramping up their suppression efforts through bogus fraud claims. They'd been employing these strategies for years, of course, but the fact that the Big Lie was being pushed by the man in the Oval Office gave it legitimacy among the Republican electorate and provided cover for any Republican officials willing to take advantage of the manufactured uncertainty.

Some Republicans made anodyne comments about giving Donald a chance to let the process make its way through the courts, with then–Senate majority leader Mitch McConnell claiming he was "100 percent within his rights" to turn to the legal system to challenge the outcome. As usual, privately they fretted over his outrageous behavior while publicly supporting his right to challenge the results. They suggested that his completely baseless claims had some legitimacy. All the while, they walked a fine line between casting doubt on Donald's loss and embracing Republican victories in some contests in both the House and the Senate. Apparently only the *presidential* election was suspect, even though voters used the same ballots for the presidential and down-ticket races.

None of their arguments was made in good faith. The Republicans had no delusions about the integrity of the election or the veracity of Donald's claim. But in deciding whether or not to back the Big Lie, and to what degree, the Republican Party asked itself one question: "How much longer can we win elections in which everybody is allowed to vote, given the way demographics in the country are trending?" The answer to that question was obviously not a date in the future.

The only thing that surprised me about Donald's defense during his second impeachment trial is that he didn't claim double jeopardy; after all, the January 6 insurrection was merely an extension of the original crime of trying to steal the election, and he'd already been tried once and acquitted. Meanwhile, the jury was composed of victims of the assault as well as, much like in the days of Jim Crow, perpetrators and accomplices. Mitch McConnell had had his eyes on the Georgia Senate runoffs scheduled for January 5, in which two Democratic newcomers had a historic chance to unseat two Republicans, and he needed to keep the base intact and angry. Senators like Texas's Ted Cruz and Missouri's Josh Hawley saw a chance to become the next standard-bearer in preparation for presidential runs in 2024; if conspiring to incite an insurrection was the best way to position themselves, so be it.

Whether or not Donald actually believed he had won doesn't really matter. As is often the case with him, he could both believe and not believe, sometimes at the same time, just as sometimes he knew he was lying about having won and sometimes he thought he was telling the truth. What's almost certain is that, until the morning of President Biden's inauguration, Donald thought he had a shot at overturning the election results. The insurrection had given him a much-needed boost, as had the fact that his party, with the exception of the ten House Republicans who'd voted to impeach him, had let him get away with having incited it.

As much as Donald was a symptom of a long-worsening disease in the body of the Republican Party, one of his unique contributions was the laying bare of incivility. People like Cruz and Hawley were free to be as horrible publicly as they've always reportedly been privately. No filter, no need to pretend anymore that they care about democracy. They could be as open as they dared about their desire to make sure, through extreme gerrymandering and voter suppression, that Black and Brown people don't have any rights, or that through regressive legislation and a stacked judiciary LGBTQ people and women don't have any rights. The precedent had been set. Donald didn't just break things. He left a road map.

The problem for Republicans, however, is that now that they've been given permission, what do they need Donald for? In fact, the last thing in the world Hawley, Cruz, and McConnell want is for Donald to run again. But by enabling and covering for Donald every step of the way, they made it possible for him to retain power—and it turns out that the power he has is over them. Donald didn't threaten to form a rival political party because he had any interest in doing that. The threat gave him leverage over Republican senators heading into the second impeachment trial. It would continue to give him leverage as long as he managed to stay relevant and they wanted to keep running for office. They are tied to him, not because he did anything for them, but because he accepted their fealty.

Despite the violence, violation, and death that occurred during the January 6 insurrection, of the dozen or so senators who had called Biden's win into question since it had been announced—including Kelly Loeffler, who campaigned on the Big Lie in the run-up to Georgia's run-off election—seven voted in favor of rejecting Pennsylvania's results and six voted in favor of rejecting Arizona's.

As early as December 2020, Josh Hawley announced his decision to commit sedition against the United States, saying, "I cannot vote to certify the electoral college results on January 6 without raising the fact that some states, particularly Pennsylvania, failed to follow their own state election laws." In a typically fact-free bit of hypocrisy, he continued, "And I cannot vote to certify without pointing out the unprecedented effort of mega corporations, including Facebook and Twitter, to interfere in this election, in support of Joe Biden." Anybody who was paying attention to social media during both the 2016 and 2020 elections would know the brazenness of Hawley's lie. In the days after the insurrection Hawley raised a million dollars off his role in the attempt to overturn the results of a legitimate election. And that's part of the problem, too: Republicans continue to monetize Donald's lies for their own purposes.

In a 2019 poll, 53 percent of Republicans ranked Donald J. Trump as a better president than Abraham Lincoln. A caller to C-SPAN, explaining his rationale, said, "Lincoln only freed the slaves. Yes, that's a big thing. But what Trump is doing is far greater." As is often the case with Donald's supporters, no concrete examples or specifics were given. Like him, they think that everything he does is always just great. Fifty-six percent of Republicans believe Donald bears no responsibility for the insurrection.

The immediate impact of what he says or does is less problematic than the precedent he sets for future politicians, particularly on the right, and the example he sets for people inclined to follow him. (Although telling people in all seriousness to inject bleach will obviously have immediate real-world implications among those who take his advice.) Suddenly, it became OK to run for higher office without releasing your tax returns and without divesting from businesses, even if they directly and indirectly benefit from the office you hold. Even more troubling was the message he sent that he was within his rights to use his platform as the most powerful person on the planet to attack private citizens and career civil servants simply because they were exercising their First Amendment rights or up-holding their duties to the Constitution. He took those rights and duties as a challenge to his authority and his impunity. He believed that he could use his extraordinary powers to cover up his crimes.

While it's obvious that white is the default in America, what might be less obvious is that Protestantism is implied in our whiteness. Essentially, "real" Americans are not just white, they are Protestants. As such, white Protestants are overrepresented in government, and are disproportion-ately represented in Congress. Currently 77 percent of Congress is made up of whites, compared with 60 percent of the general population, and 55 percent of Congress identify as some kind of Protestant, compared with 43 percent nationally.

People at the highest levels of government, like Secretary of State Mike Pompeo and Vice President Mike Pence, adhere to fundamentalist evangelical and Dominionist dogma, which is the "belief that Christians are biblically mandated to control all earthly institutions until the second coming of Jesus," as Daniel Burke wrote in the *Huffington Post*. They also sought to impose it politically. This dogma is the end of a long arc that extends from the influence of the Puritan ethos on early America and the associated impulse toward anti-intellectualism and anti-elitism (in the sense of elite as expert). It is the enemy of an open society that embraces diversity and plurality of thought, and yet it is a main driver of the Re-publican Party's trend toward fascism.

Whites assume, correctly, that without maintaining their whiteness, they would lose power, privilege, and status, and they've never been able to imagine how dismantling the system of white supremacy might compensate them for the loss of those things. The idea that living in a country that is more just and fair for all people might be of benefit to you remains elusive if you are unaware of the structural inequality that exists to benefit you in the first place. Instead, the problem of racism is viewed as a zero-sum game—not that most white people would acknowledge it in this way, but the bottom line is that the power, privilege, and status that accrue from being white in America disappear if racism does, too. When police murder Black children and no charges are filed, no one even gets fired or loses their pension, or on those rare occasions when those responsible are brought to trial and acquitted in the face of sometimes overwhelming evidence, that's not a sign that the system is broken—no, that is a sign that the system is operating in exactly the toxic way it was designed, to uphold the two tenets that have shaped America: white supremacy and the infallibility of power.

White people are not a homogenous group; they span and they represent a broad spectrum of beliefs and ideologies, from the Proud Boys on one end to antiracists on the other. But no matter where somebody falls, those who identify as white still have the power, privileges, and benefits of whiteness. Whether they want them or not, whether they are aware of them or not, at birth they automatically possess these privileges and benefits and the power that attaches to them simply because they are white.

Seventy-four million people voted for Donald in 2020. This number is mind-boggling. It only makes sense if we refuse to believe that the constituents of the modern Republican Party voted for him with their eyes wide open and understood exactly what they were voting for.

The term "base" is thrown around to describe the core group of supporters for both parties. Besides implying their equivalence, call-

whole days, and to dispel the notion that he was weak for having contracted a virus that he had spent most of the year denying. As the SUV approached, one man in the crowd shouted, "Oh my gosh, I love you! There he is, there he is! There he is!" Then, more forcefully, he said, "God bless our president. I will die for him. I will die for that man, happily. I will die for him. Anybody want to mess with him, you mess with me first. He is a hero, that man," which says much more about the state of mind of Donald's followers than it does about the man himself. The psychologist Robert Jay Lifton coined the phrase "malignant normality" to describe this phenomenon, in which people begin to see their lives and culture through the lens of the person in power. In other words, their experience and understanding of the world become unmoored from reality and cohere around the narrative proffered by somebody like Donald, a narrative that is both self-serving to him and destructive to them.

The United States Senate is one of the institutions that has been most damaged in recent years. The four years of the Trump administration are notable for the breadth of the damage caused and the depth of the cynicism that inspired it. The mastermind of the damage, Mitch McConnell, will come to be considered one of the greatest traitors to this country since Robert E. Lee, with this difference—McConnell has been trying to take us down from within.

More perhaps than any other politician, Mitch McConnell has torpedoed the notion that, above all, his job and the job of his colleagues is to serve the American people. He's earned—and embraced—the nickname "The Grim Reaper," because of the frequency with which he has killed measures sent to the Senate by the Democratic-controlled House. Instead, even in his reduced role as minority leader, his compulsive drive

ing the core of Republican voters "the base" elides a description of the kind of people who comprise the base. At one end of the spectrum are the unrepentant fascists and unreconstructed white supremacists like the Proud Boys, who currently represent the views of many if not most elected Republicans. We've known this since the 2017 Charlottesville Unite the Right protest against the removal of a Robert E. Lee statue, which resulted in the murder of counterprotester Heather Heyer. The fundamental problem wasn't that Donald called Nazis who chanted "blood and soil" and "Jews will not replace us" very fine people, it was that there were no consequences for his doing so. Nobody from his administration resigned in protest and nobody from his party demanded his resignation. His shout-out to the Proud Boys during the first 2020 presidential debate—"stand back and stand by"—was just another reminder of how explicit the rightward shift of the party now is.

On the other end of the spectrum are the low-information, knee-jerk Republican voters. In general, people are unlikely to switch political parties over the course of their lifetimes, and party affiliation is more important than the party platform. Regardless of how far from the mainstream Republican ideology becomes, it is always a better bet than the "Marxist," "socialist," liberal Democratic Party.

In between these two extremes fall the "I've got mine" people, whose notion of what is good is what is good for them, and the authoritarian-leaning voters who prefer the status quo and are made uncomfortable by diversity. And then there are one-issue voters—taxes, abortion—who can't be swayed by any other considerations, such as the candidacy of an unfit racist, misogynistic autocrat in the making.

Many of the seventy-four million choose to ignore the evidence that liberal policies work or that they themselves do better under Democratic leadership. Instead, they are convinced by outlets like Fox News and Newsmax that they should be afraid—of immigrants, of demographic changes, of socialism, and of universal health care. Fear can make people easy to manipulate, but it's an uncomfortable feeling, so Fox News hosts like Sean Hannity and Tucker Carlson stoke their viewers' outrage by focusing incessantly on nonexistent threats like the War on Christmas, or by priming them for violence against parents who have their children wear masks to protect them from COVID. On the one hand, this serves the purpose of increasing their viewers' susceptibility to conspiracy theories; on the other, it increases the likelihood that their viewers will vote against their own self-interests, which has been the goal of the Republican Party for at least four decades—all because of a false identification with a glorious past that never existed and the ancillary benefits they receive for being white.

On January 6, Confederate flags and Nazi symbols were on display, in homage to the man who had been stoking white grievance for four years, in the halls of *our* Congress, in an effort to impede the peaceful transfer of power. This was not performative—their rage, their violence, and their threats were real. Their belief in the injustice they had suffered—that the votes of women, Blacks, Jews, and LGBTQ people were allowed to count—matched their belief in the delusion that is white supremacy.

The symbolism—of the flags, of the Camp Auschwitz T-shirts—is not lost on them. They're not confused about the Lost Cause, or what happened in the Nazi concentration camps. They know what they champion. They don't just tolerate the barbarity, they revel in it. And they were willing to murder the vice president of the United States to advance their white supremacist, antidemocratic agenda.

Because of how thoroughly we've equated "good," "privilege," and "power" with whiteness, people would rather identify with slavers who tortured, raped, murdered, terrorized, dismembered, and incinerated Blacks because of the color of their skin than with the people who were brutalized by their enslavers.

That's part of the ethos that Donald tapped into, the idea that your (white) rights are more important than everybody else's. There is a disconnect on the right between what's actually good for people and this insistence on keeping everything exactly as it was in the 1950s. That's why Donald promised to preserve the coal industry, while protecting his followers from the evils of solar power and "cancer-causing" windmills. Again, this idea has been the cornerstone of the Republican Party going back to Reagan, who removed the solar panels Jimmy Carter had installed from the White House roof. Why would you go to that much trouble, take a step backward, just to score a political point? It's pandering to people who don't seem to understand why they're being pandered to.

In this way, the leader's contempt for his followers becomes a method of control that is slowly accrued through microaggressions (like abandoning them at rallies in either the freezing cold or blistering heat) that build to situations in which they literally risk their lives to appease the unappeasable ego of their leader. The rallies Donald staged in the months preceding the 2020 election were superspreader events in which his followers were expected to crowd together, shouting, often unmasked, while he stood safely apart.

In a stunning (even for him) display of sadism, Donald got into a sealed SUV with two Secret Service agents so he could wave to the crowd of his supporters that had gathered outside Walter Reed Hospital, where he was being treated for COVID. The display was necessary for him to feed his need for attention, which he'd been deprived of for two

for power merely seeks partisan advantage and partisan victories, betraying the whole concept of governance.

It has to be pointed out, however, that McConnell's project has been carried out within the system as it exists. It's unlikely that the founders explicitly designed the government of the United States to be used against itself. But McConnell, who appears to be motivated by a desire for raw power and the prospect of establishing minority rule, undoubtedly doesn't care what the founders or anybody else would think.

In an incisive description of McConnell's unique awfulness, author Robert Schlesinger writes in a piece for NBC News that he "is the living, breathing, calculating face of everything that is wrong with our current politics. To the extent to which our system has become dysfunctional, McConnell is the single chief architect of that sclerosis. Donald Trump is a dangerous, blundering wrecking ball, but McConnell was undermining the system well before (and is likely to outlast) him."

In addition, we are living in a time in which the minority has an outsized percentage of power in the federal government. Currently, the Senate is divided fifty-fifty. The fifty Republican senators represent a population that comprises approximately forty-one million fewer citizens than the Democrats represent.

Senator Joe Manchin, likely the only Democrat alive who could win a statewide election in West Virginia, currently finds himself uniquely positioned to block any legislation in the Senate because of his demands for bipartisanship and his unwillingness to do away with an antiquated, racist procedural rule known as the filibuster, which allows any senator or group of senators to block a vote unless sixty of their colleagues vote to stop debate. With the Senate evenly split, and in the current political climate, that is an almost impossible feat. But unless Manchin is willing to vote with his party on particularly divisive issues, he can essentially hold President Biden's entire agenda hostage. It is also notable that Manchin is one of two senators representing a state that has a population of 1.79 million people, or one-twenty-second of California's population. West Virginia is also 93.5 percent white and hardly representative of the American electorate. And yet Manchin is able single-handedly to stymie legislation—on gun safety, infrastructure, or voting rights—favored by 70 percent of the American people.

It isn't that our leaders fail to learn from history. Some of the leaders we choose, particularly among the Republicans, learn exactly the wrong lessons: that they can, with impunity, and within the bounds of the system governing this country, engage in antidemocratic, counter-majoritarian tactics that increase the power of the minority to impose its will on the rest of us. As it turns out, it's the tyranny of the minority we have to worry about.

This system can only fix itself. If it's corrupt or if the majority in power is the thing that needs to be fixed, then nothing is going to happen. This is the situation in which we now find ourselves. Eight sitting senators repeated and promulgated the Big Lie right up until the insurrection and beyond. They are seditionists and should have been immediately removed from office and put on trial for treason. Yet they continue to sit in the United States Senate, crafting laws and voting on legislation that will shape the future of a democracy they no longer believe in or support. There are hundreds of people in the same position in the House of Representatives. Any government that doesn't have the means to remove provable traitors can't succeed in the long run.

Donald is an instinctive fascist who is limited by his inability to see beyond himself. Or, as the historian Timothy Snyder puts it, "His vision never went further than a mirror." Still arguing about whether or not to call Donald a fascist is the new version of the media's yearslong struggle to figure out if they should call his lies lies. What's more relevant now is whether the media—and the Democrats—will extend the label of fascism to the Republican Party itself.

Donald's administration used an array of tools to coerce or co-opt government officials, many of them experts in their fields, to undermine, dismantle, and pervert our government institutions, turning them away from their mission to represent and help the American people. In this way they were able to repurpose them or, as Robert Jay Lifton would say, "Nazify" them. We cannot downplay this threat. It must be faced head-on, with eyes wide open. To downplay it, to ignore it, is to open the door to worse.

Donald was incompetent, but others in Donald's administration were anything but. What they built was a lean and ruthless machine for advancing fascism. With the help of some luck, complicit institutions, an unprepared media, and a party of willing converts, that machine largely succeeded.

CHAPTER 8

The Long Shadow

By the time I was a sophomore in college, I knew more about the Holocaust than I did about the genocide of Native Americans and the complete oppression of enslaved Africans and their subsequent generations in my own country. The message I'd received through most of my years at school, and my life in general, was that Black American history was not my history, and it was not "our" history, but something separate, other. Toni Morrison wrote, "In this country American means white. Everybody else has to hyphenate." And as a white person, it has been so easy for me to remain unaware of that, to fall in line with the prevailing and self-serving wisdom that the election of one Black president after an unbroken stretch of forty-three white presidents before him was enough to undo centuries of underrepresentation and misrepresentation. The line from slavery through Jim Crow to the overlapping crises of mass incarceration of Black men and the epidemic of police murders of innocent Black men, women, and children remains unbroken—a line largely unacknowledged by those who have the luxury of pretending that such injustices don't have any impact on their lives.

In a recent *Washington Post* op-ed in support of reparations, Gary Abernathy spoke of his previous disdain for the whole concept: "Like most conservatives, I've scoffed at the idea of reparations or a formal apology for slavery. I did not own slaves, so why would I support my government using my tax dollars for reparations or issuing an apology? Further, no one in the United States has been legally enslaved since 1865, so why are Black people today owed anything more than the same freedoms and opportunities that I enjoy?" Abernathy describes what is still a commonly held position among Americans across political affiliations and races, only 20 percent of whom favor reparations as a partial antidote to centuries of discrimination.

Part of this reluctance might be linked to the fact that, generally speaking, the story of America is told in a way that preserves the color divide. The narrative promoted about the American civil rights movement—simple, linear, with obvious heroes—stands in stark contrast to the almost nonexistent narrative about the legions of white men and women, private citizens and legislators, who used any means at their disposal—from the Senate filibuster and threats of intimidation to the most vicious acts of violence and domestic terrorism—to impede the progress of the fight for civil rights. It is as if civil rights activists were combating a system entirely devoid of actors, other than a few public figures like George Wallace, Bull Connor, and David Duke, rather than a large population of people in every walk of life. It is a whitewashed story for easy consumption that, more than anything else, is designed to make white people feel good about themselves. It avoids having to tell the tumultuous and often brutal history by carefully selecting its heroes, downplaying the tactics, ignoring the catalysts, shrouding in mystery the contributions of whites to Jim Crow, and disappearing all but the most obvious villains.

When Rosa Parks was arrested after refusing to give up her seat in the "colored" section of a public Montgomery, Alabama, bus to a white person when the "whites only" section was full, she became a symbol of nonviolent resistance. But the Montgomery bus boycott was neither the beginning nor the end of anything, for civil rights or for Rosa Parks herself. First of all, resistance to Jim Crow had been increasing since the end of World War II; second, the backlash by the white community after the U.S. District Court ruled that Alabama's bus segregation was unconstitutional was severe and, in the short term at least, did not have the desired impact. The white response was typically savage. Snipers shot at buses carrying Black passengers and five Black churches were bombed. The seven Klansmen tried for the bombings were all acquitted. Just as with *Brown v. Board of Education*, the Supreme Court decision ruling that racial segregation of children in public schools was unconstitutional, the bus segregation ruling was followed by the entrenchment and flaunting of white power.

As for Parks, she was fired from her department store job. By 1957, she had to move out of state with her family because she was unable to find new employment in Montgomery. For several years afterward she continued to receive death threats. Her involvement in the civil rights movement was much more complex than that one act of civil disobedience. She had been secretary of the Montgomery chapter of the NAACP, and she worked in the Black Power movement alongside many others, including Robert F. Williams and Malcolm X, both of whom she befriended. Williams, an advocate for arming Blacks for the purposes of self-defense and the protection of civil rights activists from Ku Klux Klan terrorism, founded the Black Armed Guard, which had approximately sixty members. On October 5, 1957, when the Ku Klux Klan threatened Dr. Albert Perry, vice president of the Monroe, North Carolina, chapter of the NAACP, Williams and the Guard set up a barrier of sandbags in front of Perry's house and, when cars full of Klan members drove by and started shooting, Williams and his men shot back. In response, the Monroe City Council banned the Klan from having motorcades.

Years later, speaking at Williams's funeral, Parks said that she had always admired him "for his courage and his commitment to freedom. The work that he did should go down in history and never be forgotten." Her presence at Williams's funeral and her remarks belie her depiction as the genteel Black woman who quietly started a movement.

But who were the antagonists in these scenarios? Who were the terrorists firebombing Black churches and lynching innocent Black people? Who were the cops who stood by or joined in? They remain elusive, perhaps because the cause they were fighting for, the reason they committed their atrocities—namely segregation and maintaining the status quo of racial inequality—was embraced by a significant minority of politicians in both the House and the Senate.

After the Civil Rights Act of 1964 was passed by the House, then–majority leader Mike Mansfield had to bypass the Judiciary Committee and bring the bill directly to the Senate floor because James Eastland, the chair of Judiciary, a fellow Democrat, and a segregationist, would never have allowed it to survive. In the end, twenty-seven senators—including twenty-one Democrats—voted against passage of the Civil Rights Act. Many of them, including Strom Thurmond, who had staged the longest filibuster in the Senate's history in an effort to kill an earlier civil rights bill in 1957, switched to the Republican Party after the bill's passage.

So the path to the Civil Rights Act was neither simple nor straightforward. Like much of the fight for Black equality, it was fraught with crimes of violence, untold violation of rights and loss of property and opportunity, and very little accountability.

After 350 years, Blacks had achieved full equality and a guarantee that their rights would be protected, at least on paper. But American ingenuity is never more ingenious than when new finding ways to promote white supremacy.

The discrimination itself has never stopped—it's just morphed into more subtle, more palatable forms of expression. Even if the thrust of some policies shifted more toward equity and inclusion, the results of decades-old government actions vis-à-vis housing, education, and criminal justice continue to have an impact on the day-to-day lives of Blacks and the opportunity gaps that still confront them. The Federal Reserve released data in early 2021 that show the average net worth of white families is 700 percent higher than that of Black families. By almost every metric—such as environmental pollution, exposure to climate risk, access to adequate and unbiased health care, and quality education—Black Americans continue to be greatly disadvantaged compared to their white counterparts.

Our very highway system is racist, not only because highway design in the 1950s destroyed Black neighborhoods, often by leveling them to make room for roads, but also because it prevented Blacks and other people of color from enjoying common resources whites take for granted. For example, Robert Moses, the architect of much of New York City's infrastructure and, according to his biographer Robert Caro, "the most racist human being I had ever really encountered," kept the bridges on Long Island parkways deliberately low so that buses carrying working-class Blacks and Hispanics, who were less likely to own cars at the time than whites, wouldn't be able to travel to the beaches.

There is also a form of environmental terrorism being carried out because of those decades-old decisions. Predominantly Black neighborhoods situated next to intercity highway systems, including Virginia Park, Detroit, where Rosa Parks moved after Montgomery, are disproportionately affected by exposure to particulate matter. According to a study published in the journal *Science Advances* and discussed in *The Washington Post* in April 2021, such exposure kills between eighty-five thousand and two hundred thousand Americans prematurely every year.

Additionally, 26 percent of all Blacks and 28 percent of all minorities live within three miles of a Superfund site. Low-income communities suffer more from heat waves because they have fewer trees and green spaces and are, therefore, hotter.

Dr. Joy DeGruy identifies high levels of stress, self-doubt, and problems with aggression and interpersonal relationships among Blacks as the fallout from post-traumatic slave syndrome. Anger, in particular, is insidious and pervasive, and can be experienced on a personal level due to thwarted ambition, but also communally by Black Americans as the result of not being able to achieve the goal of fully integrating into a society that continues to shut them out. *Everything* is seen through the prism of color.

There continues to be an interaction between the unhealed wounds of the past and wounds inflicted daily on Black Americans in every sphere and circumstance of social and civic life. The impacts are devastating. David Williams, a professor at the Harvard T. H. Chan School of Public Health, has developed the Everyday Discrimination Scale to assess the frequency with which people experience being discriminated against in various settings. There is a direct correlation between high levels of discrimination and increased risk of heart disease, diabetes, and asthma. Health care for Blacks is often substandard, a trend that is partly driven by implicit biases held by medical professionals, which are to some degree the direct result of their training, where false ideas about the physiology of Black Americans (the myth about their high tolerance for pain, for example) persist.

The cumulative result of this health crisis is the stunning revelation by Williams that two hundred Black Americans die prematurely every day. And that was before COVID-19.

This country has been dealing with drugs and addiction since its inception, but it wasn't until Richard Nixon declared drugs "public enemy number one," in 1971, that the war started. A war on drugs makes as much sense as a war on terror, but thanks to misguided legislation and reallocation of resources, the "war on drugs" went from being a catch-phrase to being a reality—at least in inner cities and communities of color—complete with SWAT teams and heavily armed, and increasingly empowered, local police.

Nixon's administration actually did, at least at the beginning, focus attention on drug treatment and rehabilitation, but the approach became increasingly punitive. The question remains whether Nixon's drug policies were purposefully crafted to target Blacks and anti-war liberals excessively. There is no doubt, however, that over time, particularly during Ronald Reagan's eight years in office, strategies devised to fight the "war on drugs" were really means to entrap Black men—with increasingly disastrous consequences.

Under Reagan, the budget for the drug war increased more than tenfold and took Nixon's measures to a whole new level. The euphemistically named Anti–Drug Abuse Act of 1986 enacted even more harsh sentences for most drugs, including marijuana. Federally mandated minimums were set at five years for five hundred grams of cocaine and the same term for only five grams of crack, despite the fact that crack has been shown to be no more dangerous than powdered cocaine. Under these guidelines, sentences were determined by statute, so judges had no leeway when it came to imposing them. Because of this act, prosecutors utilized extensive powers to coerce guilty pleas from defendants in exchange for more lenient sentencing. As of 2015, approximately 95 percent of prosecutors in the country were white.

By 2003, Blacks comprised 80 percent of the defendants federally sentenced for crack possession, even though only 30 percent of crack cocaine users were Black. Sixty-six percent of crack cocaine users in the United States were white or Hispanic. In an analysis of the arrest data provided by the FBI, Human Rights Watch found that "in every year between 1980 and 2007, arrests for drug possession have constituted 64 percent of all drug arrests. From 1999 through 2007, 80 percent or more of all drug arrests were for possession." From 1980 to 2007, Blacks were 2.8 to 5.5 times more likely to be arrested on drug charges than whites. One of the most shocking statistics is highlighted by Jeremy Travis in his book *But They All Came Back*: In the year 2000, the incarceration rate for Blacks for all crimes was twenty-six times what it had been in the 1980s. Because there is very little variability by race in terms of who uses drugs or what drugs people use, these data clearly demonstrate the inevitable result of racist drug policies and sentencing guidelines.

As has so often been the case, the Supreme Court's role in erring on the side of undermining the Constitution, failing to protect the vulnerable, and empowering antidemocratic legislation was in full force in the wake of the Anti–Drug Abuse Act. In a series of rulings devastating to protections afforded by the Fourth Amendment against unreasonable search and seizure, ignoring the purpose of the Constitution's original text (as the Court's so-called originalists often do), the power of the police to engage in such searches was expanded past the point of absurdity, until there was little need for them to show probable cause.

It all seems designed essentially to criminalize Blackness. The impact is difficult to quantify on a human level, but the statistics are mind-boggling. In 1986, federal drug sentences were 11 percent higher for Black Americans than whites. By 1990, after the Anti–Drug Abuse Act had been in place for four years, that average was 49 percent higher. The goal of mass incarceration of Black men appears to have been premeditated.

At the turn of the twentieth century, an arrest for loitering could condemn a Black man to a life of hard labor on a cotton plantation or in a turpentine forest. There was no recourse, no appeal, and almost never any relief. After the passage of the 1986 act, Black men and women, often imprisoned for similarly minor infractions or because they got caught up in an inefficient and callous system that forced plea bargains, found their lives forever shadowed by the shame of being labeled an ex-con.

Politicians could no longer get away with turning loitering into a serious felony deserving of a life sentence, but by declaring a war on drug users and falsely claiming that some drugs, like crack, were more dangerous than other drugs and used predominantly by Blacks, the means were justified. The increasingly militarized approach of law enforcement and the extreme sentences sought by prosecutors perpetuated this lie.

Thanks in part to our Puritan roots, our justice system has always been more about punishment than rehabilitation—and *it doesn't work*. The results, as measured by resources squandered and lives destroyed, have been catastrophic. And at almost every point along the way, Blacks are unfairly targeted, more likely to be charged with more serious crimes, and much more likely to serve longer sentences than their white counterparts.

All of this is bad enough. But in America, at least for certain segments of the population, there is no such thing as serving your time. The price is never paid. The hurdle placed between a felon and the ability to participate fully in civic life, the possibility of living a life of dignity and prosperity, is, much more often than not, insurmountable. Even if the alleged crime was a minor drug offense, and even if the accused pleaded guilty only in order to avoid an excessive sentence, life after prison is a continuation of the nightmare. As Michelle Alexander writes in *The New Jim Crow,* "Once you're labeled a felon, the old forms of discrimination—employment discrimination, housing discrimination, denial of the right to vote, denial of educational opportunity, denial of food stamps and other public benefits, and exclusion from jury service—are suddenly legal."

Plus ça change . . .

On the face of it, the "broken windows" theory, developed by the criminologist George L. Kelling and the political scientist James Q. Wilson, seems uncontroversial, reasonable even: obvious signs of decay and disorder can lead to more disorder until things spiral out of control. In the context of law enforcement, the hypothesis was that if local police, especially in urban areas (read: inner cities; read: ghettos), clamp down on minor crimes, more serious ones can be prevented. Taking these small infractions seriously would, theoretically, have the effect of creating an atmosphere of order, thereby promoting more lawful behavior. Basically, signs of crime lead to crime.

The broken windows theory appealed to many politicians and law enforcement officers of all stripes. The Columbia University law professor Bernard Harcourt described the reaction to the policy this way:

"It seemed like a magical solution. It allowed everybody to find a way in their own mind to get rid of the panhandler, the guy sleeping on the street, the prostitute, the drugs, the litter, and it allowed liberals to do that while still feeling self-righteous and good about themselves."

The newly elected mayor of New York City, Rudolph Giuliani, and his police commissioner, William Bratton, were enthusiastic adopters of the broken window policy in the mid-1990s. Almost as soon as Giuliani came into office, it went into effect, and misdemeanors such as public drinking, jaywalking—literally crossing the street at the wrong place—painting graffiti, and loitering were criminalized. Turnstile jumping—subway fare evasion—was considered a huge problem by the Metropolitan Transit Authority at the time, and hundreds of police officers fanned out through subway stations across the five boroughs to arrest offenders. This was the law enforcement equivalent of classifying marijuana as a gateway drug for heroin.

The perceived success of broken windows policing played a big role in Giuliani's reelection in 1997, but ultimately it was as illusory as the undeserved reputation he garnered after the terrorist attacks on September 11, 2001. It also turns out, according to a study by the sociologists Robert J. Sampson and Stephen W. Raudenbush, that "observed disorder predicts perceived disorder, but racial and economic context matter more." In other words, neighborhoods that are poor or Black or both are perceived to be more disordered than other neighborhoods even when they are not.

Broken windows policing in New York seems to have had no impact on crime rates overall. Although they did go down, this was a nationwide trend following a period of significantly high crime rates. This was not a matter of cause and effect. The actual impact was the increase in contact between the police and young (mostly) Black (mostly) men, which almost inevitably led to arrests for minor infractions like turnstile jumping. Once one is in the system, as we've seen, it becomes difficult to extricate oneself from it.

There are many failures in the way we teach our children, most fundamentally about themselves and each other. Imposing a broken windows approach on schools has had a devastating impact on those lessons. In practical terms, addressing structural problems would have made perfect sense—a well-ordered, intact physical environment can increase a child's sense of safety and self-worth, which in turn can enhance learning. But as with law enforcement, the misapplication of the practice to schools ended up with administrators and teachers treating children as if *they* were the broken windows.

Suddenly, relatively minor offenses were treated with a previously unheard-of severity. Students were being expelled for cutting class or talking back. School suspensions are supposed to be based on a set list of rules, yet, as a mammoth Texas study of over one million schoolchildren found, 97 percent of suspensions were at the administration's discretion and not based on the rules. As Libby Nelson and Dara Lind reported for *Vox*, Black students "were 31 percent more likely to receive a discretionary suspension, even after controlling for 83 other variables."

This picture got worse when actual police officers began to be deployed to public schools in the wake of the Columbine mass shooting in 1999. The original intention was to keep children safe from a similar tragedy, but over time their purpose became policing students. The number of school resource officers increased dramatically, and during the 2011–12 school year ninety-two thousand students, 31 percent of whom were Black, were arrested *in school*.

Driven by implicit bias and unaddressed prejudice, these overreactions created an environment in which the chance that students, particularly students of color, would have to interact with the criminal justice system greatly increased. The end result, of course, was that stereotypes about Blacks and criminality were reinforced and perpetuated.

The statistics again paint a stark picture of racial injustice, but they also highlight the callousness and contempt with which our system of education, its administrators, and even its educators treat our children. It becomes a self-fulfilling prophecy—children who are treated as if they are inherently bad and prone to criminality receive that message loud and clear. In this light, the problem isn't only that, according to the U.S. Department of Education Office for Civil Rights, 48 percent of preschool children who were suspended more than once are Black, it's that preschool children are suspended at all.

We teach American history (badly, for the most part) in a school system that replicates the racial disparities in the larger world. Often the content of the education itself magnifies those disparities. Only recently were dehumanizing myths about the benefits of slavery removed from textbooks. Children are not taught about the cultures and communities from which African citizens were stolen, nor about the roughly six hundred distinct Native American communities that thrived before white settlers arrived.

We separate Black American and women's literature and history as if Black Americans and women were not only outside the making of America but less important to it, a specialized subset of interest only to groups outside the majority.

There are no federally mandated guidelines for social studies or

American history curricula. The production of textbooks has become a political process that leads to wide variability from state to state in how topics crucially important to students' understanding of this country's evolution, like slavery, are taught. This lack of consensus and politicization of our history is illustrated by the recent controversy over President Biden's decision to use the 1619 Project as the basis for a grant program supporting education programs that incorporate issues of bias, discriminatory policies, and diversity in the teaching of American history.

Created by Nikole Hannah-Jones, a Pulitzer Prize–winning writer for *The New York Times*, with contributions by Jamelle Bouie, Bryan Stevenson, Kevin Kruse, and others, the 1619 Project is a necessary corrective to the ways in which most Americans understand slavery and its legacy and the contributions of Black Americans. It is, quite simply, in the words of Hannah-Jones, "an attempt to set the record straight." Although some factual inaccuracies exist in the original publication—for example, the claim that colonists fought the Revolutionary War in order to preserve slavery—the project is a vital corrective to the false notion that slavery was not inextricably bound up in the founding of this county.

Conservatives from Erik Erikson to Newt Gingrich labeled the Project "agitprop," "brainwashing," and an attempt to keep "racial tension aflame." Republican lawmakers in at least five states have threatened to cut funds from schools that use lesson plans that rely in part on the 1619 Project, which in the bills is called "racially divisive" and "revisionist." Mississippi is funding a Patriotic Education Fund and South Dakota is spending almost a million dollars to teach schoolchildren "why the U.S. is the most special nation in the history of the world." These moves have been rightly described as propaganda.

Thirty-seven Senate Republicans formally condemned President Biden's recent decision, writing, "Families did not ask for this divisive nonsense. Voters did not vote for it. Americans never decided our children should be taught that our country is inherently evil." In the choice between propaganda and truth, Republican leadership continues to make its choice clear.

Textbooks often default to euphemism. In a discussion of westward expansion and the violent confrontation with Native Americans, the American history Advanced Placement course guide includes this description: "Frontier settlers tended to champion expansion efforts, while American Indian resistance led to a sequence of wars and federal efforts to control and relocate American Indian populations." Language is never neutral—this example fails to identify the aggressors in each case and the horror of the crime.

More troubling is what's left out of many American history textbooks. While slavery is mentioned as a cause of the Civil War, and descriptions of the institution have become more blunt and realistic, larger discussions about the myriad ways in which slavery shaped America and its people or its lasting impact on both are largely avoided. And there are few, if any, discussions about the fact that seventeen of the fifty-five delegates to the Constitutional Convention, a third of the founding fathers, were enslavers and the impact that may have had on the process of drafting the Constitution. The terms "lynching," "peonage," "Trail of Tears," "Black Codes," "turpentine forests," and "convict leasing" are nowhere to be found in the AP American history curriculum. How can any student come to grips with this country's past and its profound ongoing impact on our present without a thorough knowledge of all of those terms?

In both our cities and our schools, we all would have been better off if they'd just fixed the fucking windows.

None of this occurred in the distant past. It's happening now.

In 1996, when I was thirty-one years old, Alabama state senator Charles Davidson argued that "slavery was a family institution and civilizing influence that gave enslaved people education and the Christian religion for which those converted black southerners are most grateful today."

In 2002, Strom Thurmond, the unrepentant white supremacist and segregationist, turned one hundred years old. His birthday party was attended by then–president George W. Bush, among a roster of other political figures. Trent Lott, the Republican leader in the Senate, said in celebration, "I want to say this about my state [Mississippi]: When Strom Thurmond ran for president, we voted for him. We're proud of it. And if the rest of the country had followed our lead, we wouldn't have had all these problems over all these years, either." Segregation and Jim Crow had been part of Thurmond's platform during that campaign.

In April 2021, former Pennsylvania senator Rick Santorum, who is actually paid to spout his racist opinions on CNN, said in a speech to the Young America's Foundation, an organization of young conservatives, "We came here and created a blank slate. We birthed a nation from nothing. I mean, there was nothing here. I mean, yes, we have Native Americans, but candidly, there isn't much Native American culture in American culture."

. . .

I grew up in Jamaica, a majority-minority neighborhood in Queens, New York, in which I saw not one bit of difference between me and the people I passed by on the way to the subway. In his article "The White Space," the sociologist Elijah Anderson writes, "White people typically avoid black space, but black people are required to navigate the white space as a condition of their existence." Black people in America never forget this; white people never have to think about it. I knew this because of the circumstances of my childhood.

And yet, the N-word was used without any hint of self-consciousness in my grandparents' house. My friends' parents lowered their voices to a whisper whenever they said the word "Black," as if its mere utterance made them suspect. Whenever we drove through predominantly Black neighborhoods, the adults in front would surreptitiously lock their car doors. When entering Black spaces, whites may be self-conscious, we may even be afraid, but we are rarely in danger. I knew this, too.

My neighborhood notwithstanding, I was immersed in a culture that was white. The schools I went to were almost exclusively white, and American history was white history. Black history, if it was even mentioned, was something else. The literature I studied was white literature, and Black literature was separate. And I was a child.

Racism is something we white people inflict on our children as it was inflicted on us. It is a violence we commit against them—and as they grow up, they benefit from the same entrenched system that benefits us, because our racist, white supremacist society allows us to benefit from it. We become complacent and selfish and, in the end, just as guilty as the people, and the people before them, who did this to us. The cycle continues. Our ability to be decent and kind is stunted, our desire to belong to a broader community without fear is curtailed. It is a passive experience, until it's not. The more we exercise our privilege, the easier it gets to cross that line between doing so unconsciously and doing so because we feel entitled to it. It is so easy to get used to the luxury of forgetting and the luxury of never having to know.

This is not to make excuses or suggest that our missed opportunities, our narrow worldview, in any way mitigate the impact of our choices or the effect white behavior has on Blacks in America, but we have to acknowledge our racism before we can start to do something about it. Unacknowledged, it continues unabated, denying us opportunities for friendships, partnerships, collaborations, and experiences we might otherwise have had. Our white power and privilege come at a great emotional and spiritual cost to us as human beings. We have an identity that is limited to that power and privilege. We live in a fearful, controlling, and often violent society of our own making, and unless we take the necessary steps, we'll remain trapped by it.

White Americans worry that by acknowledging the atrocities of the past, the guilt of the actual perpetrators will somehow attach to us, while it's the failure to acknowledge those atrocities that makes us complicit. We as a nation cannot begin to heal unless we face our past head-on with complete honesty and begin to understand how our country's legacy continues to affect every aspect of our lives.

CHAPTER 9

Facing the Truth

A month or two before the 2020 election, I began to think about what might be facing us when, if, we ever emerged from COVID. At the time there was no vaccine in sight—we were still hearing it might take three years or five years or longer. It might not happen at all. At the time, two hundred thousand Americans were dead, there was no way to know when the lockdown would end, and every foray out into the world still felt like a terrible gamble.

I knew we were going to be looking at a mental health crisis the likes of which this country would be woefully unprepared for, even at the best of times. It was as if we were at war and had all been called to serve, in different capacities—from desk jobs to combat—at the same time. We were all going to be coming back at the same time, too, our health care professionals just as wounded and exhausted to one degree or another as we were.

How would we emerge after so many months—of isolation, of anguish, of government-driven division, of loss? How would we reconnect, to ourselves and everybody else? What resources would be available to the hardest-hit communities? How would we grieve after grief had been so long postponed?

Robert Penn Warren once wrote, "It takes a long time for the truth to become true." Of course, some of us are better at facing the truth than others. Some of us have had no choice but to live it. If there was one thing about the year of COVID, though, it's that regardless of where we were coming from, or how sheltered or privileged we might have been, nobody really escaped unscathed. To be human, after all, is to be always vulnerable to the experience of trauma. It's an almost unavoidable part of the human condition. We just all happened to be vulnerable at the same time. Between the loneliness of isolation and the actions of a government that seemed so willing to sacrifice us, COVID was both disaster and atrocity.

Trauma can never be outrun, but it is a human impulse to try. We resist being stuck in one place because it makes it harder to avoid our feelings, and when we're running it's so much easier to pretend we don't have any. But during the pandemic, the one thing we needed most to do in order to save our lives and the lives of those we love was stay home.

Being trapped in the place in which you're being traumatized is its own version of hell.

To be human is to be oriented in time and space. When space became constricted in a way that often felt unbearable and time ceased to behave according to the rules we've always tried to impose upon it, it often felt like we were living in a perpetual present of repetition, sameness, and a lurking terror that intruded into our dreamscapes.

We had a year of unlived experience ahead of us (although we didn't know it). The day-to-day became impossible to mark. Even our rituals—holidays, birthdays—became unmoored from the traditions we attach to them and divorced from the people who help us celebrate them, making it harder to etch them into our consciousness.

In addition to the uncertainty—which, paradoxically, worsened even as we learned more about the virus—we were stalked by the constant fear of exposure, isolation, sickness, and death.

The clinical psychologist Denise Hien says, "Stress is a part of our human condition, but when stress threatens our ability to cope, or our basic sense of identity, we call that traumatic stress." And over time, when everything we feel or think or experience gets exacerbated by the slow boil of that stress, it becomes undesirable and even impossible to stay in the moment.

Time moved differently. It collapsed upon itself; it expanded past the point of absurdity. It stopped. After a few weeks I realized that in many ways COVID time felt a lot like PTSD time. Sometimes you're in it, bound by it. And then you're not, set adrift. There are no guideposts to bring you back into the stream of linear time as we usually experience it.

Sometimes, as the days and nights ran together, they had the slippery, seductive familiarity of depression. Sometimes the thread of whatever story we told ourselves, trying to stay tethered to something solid, got lost. To get our bearings we tried to orient ourselves on a sliding scale of misfortune—to allow us to feel better or worse compared to others.

We were all exposed to trauma in varying degrees, but there was no uniformity to the ways we responded. Past was no prologue: introverts became desperate for company, extroverts developed social anxiety. Some of us became depressed or obsessive, while others developed PTSD. Some reacted with resilience. There was no way to know.

When the vaccine was announced and suddenly we were talking about months until we could be out in the world again, finally knowing *when* instead of living day to day with only the most amorphous sense of what might be in store, there was a sense of hope for the first time in a long time.

But traumatic time destroys in both directions—past and future—and the truth of that can be hard to face, especially for the unpracticed. Being yanked so suddenly back into time forced us to reckon with the fact that six months, no matter how you count it, is a very long time. We knew there was an end in sight, but how would we get there? And who would we be when we did?

The pull to forget is even stronger than the pull to run. Forgetting makes us complicit with the trauma we're trying to escape, and by ignoring the experience of it and, more important, the way the experience made us feel, a part of us, in some cases the most vital part of who we are, remains tethered to the past. By cutting ourselves off from that emotion we shut down access to the full range of who we are. But the price of release is steep, and it's so much easier to live our lives pretending we're whole.

Judith Herman, in *Trauma and Recovery,* quotes a Vietnam vet who said, "If at the end of a war story you feel uplifted, or if you feel that some bit of rectitude has been salvaged from the larger waste, then you have been made the victim of a very old and terrible lie."

It's remarkable how desperately we want to salvage that rectitude, as if the only way to give meaning to pain is to lie about it. It's counterproductive, of course, but it isn't just individuals who are motivated to forget. The desire to move on, especially after large-scale betrayals, is irresistible. As soon as the dust clears, the people in power tell us everything is fine; there is no need to look back. After all, what atrocities don't we want to put behind us? What crimes against humanity would we like to dredge up?

There are as many reasons to forget as there are people on the planet—guilt, shame, agony, the desperate need to avoid pain or evade responsibility, or a personally tailored mix of those. But as seductive as it is, wiping out chapters in our history, individual or collective, leaves future generations vulnerable. We know this. Only remembering will heal us. Maybe it will even set us free.

The similarities between the Wilson and Trump administrations and the ways in which they handled the 1918 and the 2020 pandemics is uncanny. President Woodrow Wilson didn't issue one public statement about influenza even as hundreds of thousands of Americans were dying. As World War I was winding down, he stubbornly refused to halt troop mobilizations, thereby allowing infections to spread both here and abroad. Both men, at least on the surface, had an obsession that kept them from being interested in the pandemic—for Wilson it was the war and for Donald it was the economy.

But perhaps the most remarkable thing about the 1918 pandemic is the silence that followed. In some ways it's as if it never happened. The only account in literature I could find is a short story by Katherine Anne Porter. Perhaps the tragedy got swallowed up by the crisis of the world war before and the catastrophe of the Depression after. Or perhaps the totality of the loss, 725,000 dead, more than we've lost today, and a much larger percentage of the population, made it impossible to process.

In contrast, there was a very clear narrative about World War II. Unfortunately, it was completely divorced from reality. Returning soldiers were valorized, the war itself cast as a triumph of good over evil, as if, at the end of the conflict, everything was just fine. Nobody talked about the broken marriages or the psych wards full of veterans suffering from serious mental disorders. The public's unwillingness to acknowledge the reality of the war or listen to the stories of what our soldiers had actually been through made it difficult, if not impossible, for them to tell those stories. Their silence made room for reinvention, and their trauma got buried. But it never went away.

That kind of neglect or cultural interdiction against speaking about one's traumatic experiences itself causes trauma. The effects don't remain isolated—trauma is impossible to compartmentalize—but they can further trap the person, or group of people, suffering in an inescapable loop of dissociation, self-loathing, and sense of futility.

Trauma is compounded when it occurs over time, during wars or pandemics, and when it undermines or obliterates one's sense of agency. When the traumatizing circumstances are made gratuitously worse by the people who (1) are responsible for them and (2) could have done something to mitigate them, the resulting sense of betrayal can feel similar to torture. Symbolically, at least, the experience is akin to being in the presence of another human being who, though witnessing the extremity of your situation, even though it could result in your death and despite having the power to render you assistance, refuses. When your life is endangered by the person who could save you, the sense of betrayal can be unbearable.

One of the worst things that was done to us during the year of COVID was the purposeful attempt to divide us and further isolate us from one another. One of the very few mitigating factors of mass trauma is the sense that we are all in it together. In times of war, for example, suicide rates go down because there is a sense of common purpose. Members of the Trump administration made that impossible not because they were incompetent but because they thought it was a winning strategy. Promoting divisiveness among us suited their purposes, just as setting up a false dichotomy between the pandemic and the economy did. In real time it could be hard to gauge how cynical and cruel this ploy was, but in retrospect the extent of the deliberate sabotage is breathtaking. It's hard to grapple with what was taken from us and even harder to fathom the depth of depravity required to do the taking.

As Elaine Scarry wrote in *The Body in Pain*, "to have great pain is to have certainty; to hear that another person has pain is to have doubt." But despite the attempts to divide us, we are all witnesses to each other's suffering. Even in isolation we have the certainty of our shared experiences.

While we can embrace that, we also have to make room for the probability that we're all going to emerge from this experience altered, with post-COVID bodies and post-COVID attitudes. We'll be self-conscious in a way we may not otherwise have been, anxious or depressed because people are going to see us as we are now, not as we were a year ago, or two years ago. Whether or not this is a bad thing depends to a large extent on how willing we are to accept the new version of ourselves, how sincerely we accept the changes, and how kind we can be to this stranger who is now us.

There will be times when we are unrecognizable to ourselves, particularly in the company of people whose relationships used to help define us. Everyday occurrences that we never had to think about—hugging a friend we haven't seen in a long time, going to a restaurant, being in a crowd—will require thought, a working out of logistics, risk-versus-reward assessments. Spontaneity will be on hold for a while.

But if we want to heal, it's important to resist calls to look to the future, not the past. The past is what shaped us. Trauma is enervating and it is entirely natural to want to move beyond it. But trauma changes us at the cellular level. We carry it with us in our bodies, and there is no moving on without facing what we want to run from, because to dismiss your own pain is to postpone your freedom from it.

As a country, we have to resist the urge to move on just as defiantly. If nothing else, a crisis of this magnitude and scope forces us to assess the structural failures that left us so vulnerable. Despite the fact that mental health care professionals have been fighting for years to destigmatize their field, we still tend to treat mental illness as an afterthought or a moral failing and mental health as a luxury. The impact of COVID on our nation's psychological and emotional well-being underscores how dangerous it is to keep making that mistake.

The impact of unacknowledged trauma can be catastrophic—at both the personal and the societal levels—and by failing to invest in the infrastructure necessary to prevent or at least mitigate these kinds of disasters in the future, we leave ourselves open to long-term damage that could be irreparable.

One of the most striking developments of the last five years has been the trend toward cruelty, the cultivation of a callousness toward anybody who believes differently or thinks differently. The mantra of "Fuck your feelings" at Donald's rallies reverberated and reminded us that, even though it goes underground from time to time, the impulse toward cruelty never completely goes away. It's hard to understand why someone would choose to withhold kindness even in moments of extreme suffering, and it continues to rankle that our need for comfort and reassurance during the last year was met not just with indifference but with contempt, as if our concerns for ourselves and each other were just another indication of how weak and unworthy we are, as if kindness can be split off from the human experience without diminishing us irrevocably. Who would want that for their children? And why would anybody choose that for themselves? Being kind doesn't make you weak. Receiving kindness doesn't render us incapable—it fortifies us.

Belittling or failing to acknowledge the importance of kindness is sociopathic. It is a by-product of the myth of rugged individualism that continues to have a place in the American psyche because it appeals to those who see benefit in convincing other people (and themselves) that they are self-made. It provides cover for those who don't have any impulse toward helping people because there is no profit in it. The fact that "individualism" in this context is a myth hasn't prevented it from exerting an outsize influence in our culture. Many of the responses to COVID—from refusing to wear a mask to entering state capitols with semiautomatic weapons—were a rejection of the idea that as citizens we don't just have rights; we have responsibilities.

A society without kindness is no more tenable than a relationship without it. For four years the performative cruelty of the Trump administration and its message that we need to be tough and vindictive and punitive wore away at the fabric of our society. We were pitted against one another and forced to choose sides.

President Biden has a rare opportunity to make some real progress toward creating structural change that addresses our blind spots on issues of psychological well-being. At the same time, by demonstrating on a grand scale how effective government can be at helping people, by demonstrating empathy, he can go a long way toward undoing the damage done by his predecessor. We can, maybe for the first time, ask ourselves: What, after all, do we owe each other?

"Liberal democracy," the behavioral economist Karen Stenner writes, "has now exceeded many people's capacity to tolerate it." Any path we take as we move on from COVID and the four years of the Trump administration needs to take that into consideration. One election isn't going to do the trick. The consensus seemed to be that the 2020 election was the most consequential in our lifetime, but, depending how the electorate trends in the next two years, it's possible that the election of 2022 or 2024 will be. The Biden administration's early commitment to restoring the safety net gives us an opening to tackle in even more direct ways the inequalities that have been built into our system since the beginning. We squander this chance at our peril.

One problem, though, is that the pendulum has always swung further to the right than to the left. Usually when a Democratic president comes in after a disastrous Republican administration, which has further eroded people's rights and destroyed the economy, the best we get is a swing back to the middle. Now we are again at the point where demanding equal rights for all our citizens is considered a liberal position. If that's the case, then that is precisely the position at which I hope the pendulum remains permanently stuck.

Fundamental change is required. Not a restructuring, but a reimagining of American potential. In the last eighteen months we have had experiences that should have given us at least some real-life, day-to-day insight into how important it is for us to be connected. By the same token, we've experienced what many Americans have been living with all their lives: what it's like to live in fear—of a government that betrays you, of neighbors who don't look out for you, of simply being out in the world.

The pandemic revealed the impact of decades' worth of inequality and racism in the immense toll it's taken on communities of color. The government's response to COVID revealed something even darker—that it was willing to exploit those inequalities in order to score political points with the Republican base.

Slavery was not our fault, we say. But whether consciously or not, we have all benefited from it in a million ways, large and largely unseen. The original sin may not be our fault, but it remains our burden. White Americans need to interrogate our assumptions about race but also examine our failures to root out white supremacy. The longer we go without recognizing that fact, the more it becomes our responsibility.

A major concern after the Civil War was that freedmen and freedwomen would become dependent on government assistance. When during Reconstruction Blacks showed that they could succeed without it, every imaginable obstacle—from denying them loans and credit and job opportunities to threats of violence and actual terrorism—was put up between them and prosperity. And yet the conclusion drawn by many politicians and newspapers in the North was that after twelve years the experiment had failed and Blacks had proven themselves unworthy of freedom. Blacks were told to pull themselves up by their bootstraps after their boots had been stolen from them.

This country was built on land stolen from its rightful owners, the native populations. This country was built on the backs and with the blood of millions of Black men and women from whom prosperity, health, and opportunity were and continue to be withheld.

Yet, like a patient with post-traumatic stress disorder who can't—or won't—face the truth of the original trauma that continues to debilitate her, this country has failed to grapple with the pain of its early history. We are, as a nation, perpetually divided and angry, rendered a shadow of what we might have been, what we may still be, because the vast majority of us can't face the truth of the origins of our privilege and the legacy of cruelty that continues to benefit us—or because we are never asked to.

Working-class whites are victims of the system, too. They have been tricked into voting against their own self-interest by a ruling class that has convinced them that allegiance to their whiteness is more valuable than health care or any other social programs that would lift them up. Superiority over Blacks, they have been told, just as the white laborers in the colonies were told, is more important than financial gain. Joining forces with the wealthy and powerful would be more beneficial symbolically, if not materially, than joining forces with the Black working class. Of course, none of that is true, but it's a compelling narrative, so much easier than facing the truth of your having been used and lied to.

If you are white in America and feel you've been left behind and shut out of the prosperity afforded to others, it's not because of Black people and immigrants. It's because the politicians you continue to vote for stoke your bigotry and sense of grievance while exploiting your ignorance in order to keep you exactly where you are—disempowered, angry, and fearful.

As the four years of the Trump administration and the first hundred days of the Biden administration demonstrated, leadership matters. Even when things are going well, however, there will be missteps.

At the end of April 2021, two Republican politicians weighed in on race in America. Tate Reeves, the governor of Mississippi, claimed there is no systemic racism in his state. (Not long before this he had declared April to be Confederate Heritage Month, as governors of that state have done for decades.) Mississippi, however, could well have had a Democratic governor and maybe even a Democratic senator if it weren't for the state's refusal to restore voting rights to former felons and its entrenched problems with voter suppression. After all, Mississippi elected the first two Black senators in this country back in the late nineteenth century. The power is there, but it's been systematically thwarted for two centuries.

Then Tim Scott, a Republican senator from South Carolina—and the only Black Republican senator—said in his rebuttal to President Joe Biden's first address to Congress that America is not a racist country.

In response to Scott, Vice President Kamala Harris also said that America is not a racist country, adding that we must "speak truth" about its history with racism. President Biden made much the same point. I would suggest that, despite the voices of civil rights activists, scholars, voters, and writers raised in opposition to oppression since the founding, it is our country's centuries-long failure not only to speak that truth but to confront it that has kept this country racist.

It's vital that we address the past, but language matters, and saying we're not racist sends the wrong message. It is the political equivalent of blaming police violence on a "few bad apples."

If we're told that we need to "speak truth" only about the past, it implies we can be complacent about the present. When our leaders tell us that America is not a racist country, whether the motive is malicious or well intentioned, the wrong people are emboldened and the rest of us are demoralized. Making that claim puts a wrench in the wheels of progress, to the extent they were even turning. It gives the side that is comfortable with the status quo permission not to do the very hard work of self-reflection, while the rest of us wonder what the hell it will take to gain enough momentum for real change to happen. If we can acknowledge there is systemic racism, then by what logic can we posit that the country governed by that system is somehow free of its racism? And if America isn't a racist country, then what does that word even mean?

This isn't a denunciation, merely an observation of fact. For our leaders to avoid being blunt about this is to miss an opportunity finally to engage with the issue nationally. To avoid the topic is to allow injustices to continue.

It's not surprising when authoritarians try to divide us against ourselves in order to accrue more power. That's what authoritarians do. It's dispiriting, though, when our leaders who purport to want to heal our country miss the opportunity to unite us. Choosing the easy path shuts down conversation, requires no sacrifices, effects no change, and in the end keeps in place the system that privileges some of us and shuts everybody else out—that's what happens when you cling to the notion that America is not a racist country.

. . .

It is almost impossible to grow up white in America and not be racist. We live in a society where white is the default. In media, white is the default. We watch news programs that disproportionately cover Black crime. We live in communities where Black people are criminalized and comprise a disproportionately high percentage of the prison population, not because they are worse than, or more violent than, or have tendencies to be more criminal than white people, but because they are arrested more. They are accused more. They are convicted more. They are sentenced more harshly.

We are a rich country in which there are ghettoes and food deserts. We use property taxes to fund public schools so children of the rich get more and children of the poor and working class get less. We have entire cities without clean water, and an entire class of people we refer to unironically as the "working poor."

Nobody should live in a slum or a ghetto. Nobody should go to a school that has chipping paint and broken plumbing, or that serves rotten food; nobody should have his or her entire future destroyed because of committing a misdemeanor. It shouldn't cost more to eat healthy food than it does to eat fast food. Yet all of these things are true because the system has been rigged since the beginning against the very people who created our wealth.

The force of white supremacy was so great that it launched America on a trajectory it often seems incapable of deviating from. The only way to combat inertia is with force. Paying out reparations will show the world, and the people from whom so much has been taken, that America is capable of basic human decency on a grand scale and is committed to fulfilling its potential as a democracy. Every society asks itself the questions, Who counts? Who doesn't? For four centuries the calculus used to answer these questions has changed, but the answers rarely have.

The United States engages in its own form of toxic positivity—a series of deep denials that perpetuates our two-tiered system, maintains double standards, and keeps our wounds from healing. This recurring urge to move on, this impatience with doing the hard work of atonement, of accountability, of tearing down the structures of oppression and rebuilding new ones that work for everybody, traps us in the same cycle of privilege and denial of privilege that keeps us separate, hostile, and suspicious.

After the votes of the 2020 presidential election were finally tallied, we were faced with another question. It wasn't about the seventy-four million of us who voted for four more years of racism and cruelty and mass death, it was about the eighty-four million of us who didn't vote for those things. After one of the worst series of crises in American history and the closest brush with fascism we've ever had, what were we going to do about it? Were we going to seize the opportunity to effect real and lasting change, or were we going to kick the can down the road again?

If everybody were equal and given the same opportunities at birth, what would I, a white American, be giving up? Not my freedom, not my vote, not my safety. I would be giving up what does not belong to me in the first place, something that is a figment that came to be transformed through the centuries into real power. I would be giving up unearned privilege and power. White superiority is a fiction, but it's so deeply ingrained that the privileges that accrue are real and have a real impact. But the problem with white privilege is that you can't give it up even if you wanted to.

In April 2021, HR 40, a bill introduced over thirty years ago by John Conyers and named in homage to General William T. Sherman's Field Order 15, which granted forty-acre plots to freedmen and -women, is wending its way through Congress as of this writing. The purpose of HR 40 is to evaluate the legacy and ongoing harm of slavery and debate the idea of reparations. Again, leadership matters, and it's probably not a coincidence that the bill finally gained traction while Biden's in the Oval Office.

If we want to create a society in which there really is equal justice for all, we've got to level the playing field and dismantle every part of the system that grants white Americans unearned privilege at the cost of oppressing others. Reparations are a way to do that. The concept is straightforward—beginning four hundred years ago, millions of men, women, and children were forcibly removed from their homes. Four hundred thousand of them were brought to the American colonies, where they were sold and forced to work for no wages. This was a permanent condition. Once enslaved, they were enslaved for life, and their children were enslaved after them. Their lives were constantly in danger and their families could be broken up at any time. By the time slavery was abolished in 1865, the number of people living in bondage in the United States had grown to four million. Every generation since has been shut out of the economic and educational benefits that were regularly bestowed on whites. There is no way to compensate for the loss of life or the destroyed potential or the fallout from the resulting traumas, but reparations will, as far as possible, return what has been stolen.

Until the playing field is leveled, America is not a democracy. Until everybody eligible is allowed to vote unimpeded, America is not a democracy. As long as a majority of the majority doesn't have a problem with the deliberate economic plunder and disenfranchisement of large swaths of the population, and as long as the rest of us ignore it— because to pay attention would be to challenge our privilege—nothing will change.

Epilogue

uilty on all three counts.

In the aftermath of the Derek Chauvin verdict, Jason Johnson, a political scientist and commentator, said, "What this says to me is that in order to get a nominal degree of justice in this country, that a Black man has to be murdered, on air, viewed by the entire world. There would have to be a year's worth of protests, and a phalanx of other white police officers to tell one white officer he was wrong, in order to get one scintilla of justice."

The Notre Dame professor John Duffy described the verdict as "a single drop of water on a tongue parched over 400 years."

It took the righteous grief and rage compounded across centuries of hundreds of thousands of Black Americans and their willingness to put their lives on the line yet again to get the attention of a system, of a country that has ignored their pain for far too long.

Recently a court in Columbus, Ohio, ruled that police can't use tear gas and rubber bullets against peaceful protesters, something that clearly does not go without saying.

On the other hand, legislators in Florida and other states have passed laws reducing the liability of people who run over peaceful protesters with their cars, which the ACLU refers to as "hit and kill" bills.

The forces, unequal but opposite, keep pushing against each other.

Black Lives Matter. Black lives matter. It's a simple enough statement. The responses—All Lives Matter, Blue Lives Matter—underscore the necessity of having to say something so essential.

To raise your voice if you are Black in America is to take an unfathomable risk. To drive your car, or use your phone, or have a picnic, or sleep in your own bed is to trigger a white fear so fundamental and so shared that to be Black in America is an almost impossible proposition.

And right now this is exactly who we are. This is exactly how things will continue to be in an America that values whiteness above everything else if we, those of us who can, refuse to make a different choice. There is no moving on from this. For once we need to dig in our heels and demand what's right, even if it hurts. Because the first step in healing is facing the truth and feeling the pain.

It's time for us to put our bodies on the line, it's time for us to listen.

It's time for us to kneel.

Acknowledgments

At St. Martin's Press thanks to Jennifer Enderlin, George Witte, Kevin Reilly, Alan Bradshaw, Greg Villepique, Adriana Coada, Michelle Mc-Millian, Michael Storrings, Nikolaas Eickelbeck, Paul Hochman, Martin Quinn, Gabrielle Gantz, and Tracey Guest.

At UTA thanks to Jennifer Roehrer, Marc Paskin, Pilar Queen, and the rest of our amazing team.

Thanks also to Athena Lark for her comprehensive and thoughtful sensitivity read; Henry Kaufman, for the legal vetting and the cartoons (!); Darren Ankstrom, fact-checker extraordinaire; Melissa Shore for her help with trauma research; David Morris for his great insights into PTSD (sorry I ghosted you); and Lachlan Cartwright for getting the ball rolling even though I wasn't remotely ready—I am now officially "Tanned, rested, and ready to go."

I am grateful to Ben Stiller and Nicky Weinstock for the incredible opportunity, to Sarah Soleimani for taking the journey with me, and to Sylvie Rabineau at William Morris Endeavor for making it happen.

Thank you to a group of extraordinary women who broadened and deepened my understanding of the dangers facing us during this critical time in our history: Ruth Ben-Ghiat, Rosa Brooks, Mieke Eoyang, Laurie Garrett, Denise Hien, Susan Opotow, Kavita Patel, and Maya Wiley.

My deep appreciation to Patti Lupone, who has inspired me since I was thirteen, for her fierce dedication to the arts and the people who make them possible; to Jane Fonda for her kindness and the work she does every day to save our planet; to Chely Wright and Lauren Blitzer for reaching out at the very beginning and giving me the chance to contribute to their amazing project; to Rob Rieman, for the invitation and his belief in my work; to David Rothkopf, not only for the great Deep State Radio and awesome Twitter threads, but for his generosity; Molly Jong-Fast for her wonderful writing and the introduction that changed everything.

To new friends who have helped make this indescribable year more bearable: Brad Berkwitt; Allison Gill; Dana Goldberg; Renee Stubbs; and Joyce Vance, E. Jean Carroll, Jennifer Taub, and Katy Phang for inviting me into the inner circle of knitting. Also, to E. Jean for her courage.

If I've missed anybody please forgive me but, because of COVID, I haven't actually met most of you. Now that we can all be in the same room, I will make it up to you—as long as you're vaccinated.

My extreme gratitude to Lynval Richardson, Claudia Baker, Tiago Sarmento and all of the Julucans for creating one of the most extraordinary experiences of my life at a time when I most needed it. It is a privilege to know you.

To Annie Champion for being an amazing friend; Ted Boutrous for his continuing support; Robbie Kaplan for being a total badass; John Quinn and Alexander Rodney for their amazing work; and Sue Craig and Russ Buettner for continuing to do extraordinary investigative journalism. Sue, I will be forever grateful that you knocked on my door.

ACKNOWLEDGMENTS

I am thankful to have reconnected with Denise Dewald, Lana Fioren-tino, Wendy Firtel, Suzanne and Brian Gillman, Judy Gold, Helene Hernes, Alan Lebowitz, Reshmi Paul, Pam Perlman, Gaby, Rocky, and Judy Richard, Suzanne Shavelson, Nicole Sherman, Kelly Sullivan, and Kate Szymanski.

Thanks as always to Denise Kemp for doing the heavy lifting; Liz Stein for getting through it, but let's just say I'm looking forward to moving on to the Unicorn; Pat Roth for being there for me; Eric Adler for his continuing friendship—I'm very glad we got to skip the pawn-broker this time around; John Barrengos for always knowing what to say; and Alice Frankston for once again getting me across the finish line.

And to my daughter, Avary, who never ceases to make me proud of who she is. I love you, Av.

A Note on Sources

As events unfolded in the months leading up to the 2020 election and then the months leading up to the second Senate impeachment trial, it became obvious that I would have to broaden my scope in order to make sense of not only how we were going to deal with our many crises but how we ended up at a point where we were so vulnerable.

To do that I read widely and deeply in order to steep myself in scholarship that provided as many perspectives as possible across many topics, including the history of Reconstruction, the Jim Crow South, the North's history of oppression and segregation, epigenetics, critical race theory, Calvinism, white supremacy, fascism, the scope of justice, the relevance of all of these to the current political moment, and many others. It turns out that making sense of twenty-first-century America in general and the last four years in particular would not have been possible otherwise.

Not all of the sources I learned so much from are cited directly in the book, but the insights, knowledge, and perspective I gained from them proved invaluable in helping me make sense of the sweep and scope of our history in a way I previously had not, as well as construct my own narrative.

For helping me understand the centrality of race, racism, white supremacy, and fascism to American history, thank you to Michelle Alexander, Theodore Allen, Elijah Anderson, Douglas Blackmon, David Blight, Ron Chernow, Richard Delgado and Jean Stefancic, Eric Foner, Henry Louis Gates, Nikole Hannah-Jones and all of the contributors to the 1619 Project, Jerrold Packard, Jason Stanley, Bryan Stevenson at the Equal Justice Initiative, and Isabel Wilkerson.

For keeping me grounded and informed (although not sanguine) about the short- and long-term consequences of the Trump administration and helping keep my eyes wide open about the dangers we still face going forward, I am grateful to Anne Applebaum, Ruth Ben-Ghiat, Charles Blow, Jamelle Bouie, Ta-Nehisi Coates, David Corn at *Mother Jones*, Masha Gessen, Ryan Goodman at *Just Security*, Sherrilyn Ifill, Ibram X. Kendi, Sarah Kendzior, Ezra Klein, Ed Luce at *The Financial Times*, Josh Marshall at *Talking Points Memo*, Malcolm Nance, Greg Sargent and Paul Waldman at *The Washington Post*, Timothy Snyder, Jacob Soboroff, Brent Staples, and David Williams.

And for helping me reach a deeper understanding of trauma and complex post-traumatic stress disorder, my thanks to Joy DeGruy, Judith Herman, and Bessel van der Kolk.

References

Alexander, Michelle. (2020). *The New Jim Crow: Mass Incarceration in the Age of Colorblindness, 10th Anniversary Edition*. New York: The New Press.

Allen, Theodore W. (2012). *The Invention of the White Race, Volume 1: Racial Oppression and Social Control (Second Edition)*. Brooklyn: Verso Books.

———. (2012). *The Invention of the White Race, Volume 2: The Origin of Racial Oppression in Anglo-America (Second Edition)*. Brooklyn: Verso Books.

Allport, Gordon W. (1958). *The Nature of Prejudice*. New York: Doubleday.

Anderson, Elijah. (2015). "The White Space." *Sociology of Race and Ethnicity* 1, 10–21.

Anderson, Michael C., and Simon Hanslmayr. (2014). "Neural Mechanisms of Motivated Forgetting." *Trends in Cognitive Sciences* 6, 279–292.

Applebaum, Anne. (2020). *Twilight of Democracy: The Seductive Lure of Authoritarianism*. New York: Doubleday.

Arendt, Hannah. (1955; reprint, 1973). *The Origins of Totalitarianism*. New York: Harcourt.

Atkinson, Meera. (2017). *The Poetics of Transgenerational Trauma*. New York: Bloomsbury USA.

Bailyn, Bernard, ed. (1993). *The Debate on the Constitution: Federalist and Antifederalist Speeches, Articles, and Letters During the Struggle over Ratification: Part One, September 1787–February 1788*. New York: Library of America.

————. (1993). *Federalist and Antifederalist Speeches, Articles, and Letters During the Struggle over Ratification: Part Two, January to August 1788*. New York: Library of America.

Baldwin, James. (1955; reprint, 1984). *Notes of a Native Son*. Boston: Beacon Press.

————. (1963; reprint, 1992). *The Fire Next Time*. New York: Vintage Books.

Barry, John M. (2005). *The Great Influenza: The Story of the Deadliest Pandemic in History*. New York: Penguin Books.

Bell, Derrick. (2008). *Faces at the Bottom of the Well: The Permanence of Racism*. New York: Basic Books.

Ben-Ghiat, Ruth. (2020). *Strongmen: Mussolini to the Present*. New York: W. W. Norton.

Blackmon, Douglas A. (2009). *Slavery by Another Name: The Reenslavement of Black Americans from the Civil War to World War II*. New York: Anchor Books.

Blight, David W. (2020). *Frederick Douglass: Prophet of Freedom*. New York: Simon & Schuster.

Briere, John. N., and Catherine Scott. (2014). *Principles of Trauma Therapy: A Guide to Symptoms, Evaluation, and Treatment, 2nd Edition (DSM-5 Update)*. Los Angeles: SAGE Publications.

Camp, Stephanie M. H. (2004). *Closer to Freedom: Enslaved Women and Everyday Resistance in the Plantation South*. Chapel Hill: University of North Carolina Press.

Chernow, Ron. (2017). *Grant*. New York: Penguin Books.

Coates, Ta-Nehisi. (2015). *Between the World and Me*. New York: One World.

Crenshaw, Kimberlé, et al., editors. (1996). *Critical Race Theory: The Key Writings That Formed the Movement*. New York: The New Press.

Crocq, Marc-Antoine, and Louis Crocq. (2000). "From Shell Shock and War Neurosis to Posttraumatic Stress Disorder: A History of Psychotraumatology." *Posttraumatic Stress Disorder* 1, 47–55.

Daniel, Pete. (1972). *The Shadow of Slavery: Peonage in the South, 1901–1969*. Champaign: University of Illinois Press.

Dean, Eric T., Jr. (1997). *Shook over Hell: Post-Traumatic Stress, Vietnam, and the Civil War*. Cambridge, MA: Harvard University Press.

DeGruy, Joy. (2017). *Post Traumatic Slave Syndrome: America's Legacy of Enduring Injury and Healing, Newly Revised and Updated Edition*. Portland, OR: Joy DeGruy Publications.

Delgado, Richard, and Jean Stefancic. (2000). *Critical Race Theory: An Introduction*. New York: New York University Press.

Douglass, Frederick. (2013). *The Complete Autobiographies of Frederick Douglass*. New York: Simon & Schuster.

DuBois, W. E. B. (1903; reprint, 2009). *The Souls of Black Folk*. New York: Library of America.

Duran, Eduardo, et al. (1998). "Healing the American Indian Soul Wound." In *International Handbook of Multigenerational Legacies of Trauma*, ed. Yael Danieli, 341–354. Boston: Springer.

Equal Justice Initiative. (2018). "Segregation in America." https://eji .org/reports/segregation-in-america/.

————. (2020). "Reconstruction in America: Racial Violence After the Civil War." https://eji.org/reports/reconstruction-in-america-overview/.

Fine, M. (2004). "The Power of the Brown v. Board of Education Decision: Theorizing Threats to Sustainability." *American Psychologist* 59 (6), 502–510.

Foner, Eric. (2015). *A Short History of Reconstruction (Updated Edition)*. New York: HarperCollins.

Fossion, Pierre, et al. (2015). "Transgenerational Transmission of Trauma in Families of Holocaust Survivors: The Consequences of Extreme Family Functioning on Resilience, Sense of Coherence, Anxiety and Depression." *Journal of Affective Disorders* 171, 48–53.

Foucault, Michel. (1995). *Discipline and Punish: The Birth of Prison*. New York: Vintage Books.

Fromm, Erich. (2013). *Escape from Freedom*. New York: Open Road Media.

Garrett, Laurie. (1994). *The Coming Plague: Newly Emerging Diseases in a World out of Balance*. New York: Macmillan.

Gates, Henry Louis, Jr. (2019). *Stony the Road: Reconstruction, White Supremacy, and the Rise of Jim Crow*. New York: Penguin Books.

Ginzburg, Ralph. (1988). *100 Years of Lynchings*. Baltimore: Black Classic Press.

Glymph, Thavolia. (2008). *Out of the House of Bondage: The Transformation of the Plantation Household*. Cambridge: Cambridge University Press.

Gould, Stephen Jay. (2006). *The Mismeasure of Man (Revised and Expanded)*. New York: W. W. Norton.

Guthrie, Robert V. (2004). *Even the Rat Was White: A Historical View of Psychology*. New York: Pearson College Division.

Haines, Staci K. (2019). *The Politics of Trauma: Somatics, Healing, and Social Justice*. Berkeley, CA: North Atlantic Books.

Hannah-Jones, Nikole, et al. The 1619 Project. *New York Times*, August 14, 2019.

Hart, Bradley W. (2018). *Hitler's American Friends: The Third Reich's Supporters in the United States*. New York: Thomas Dunne Books.

Hedges, Chris. (2009). *Empire of Illusion: The End of Literacy and the Triumph of Spectacle*. New York: Bold Type Books.

Herman, Judith L. (2015). *Trauma and Recovery: The Aftermath of Violence—from Domestic Abuse to Political Terror*. New York: Basic Books.

Hofstadter, Richard. (1963; 1966). *Anti-intellectualism in American Life*. New York: Vintage Books.

———. (1952; reprint, 2008). *The Paranoid Style in American Politics, and Other Essays*. New York: Vintage Books.

Hübl, Thomas, and Julie J. Avritt. (2020). *Healing Collective Trauma: A Process for Integrating Our Intergenerational and Cultural Wounds*. Boulder: Sounds True.

Hunt, Raymond G., and Benjamin Bowser. (1996). *Impacts of Racism on White Americans*. Los Angeles: SAGE Publications.

Johnson, Walter. (2009). *Soul by Soul: Life Inside the Antebellum Slave Market*. Cambridge, MA: Harvard University Press.

Kendi, Ibram X. (2016). *Stamped from the Beginning: The Definitive History of Racist Ideas in America*. New York: Bold Type Books.

———. (2019). *How to Be an Antiracist*. New York: One World/Ballantine.

Kendzior, Sarah. (2020). *Hiding in Plain Sight: The Invention of Donald Trump and the Erosion of America*. New York: Flatiron Books.

Klein, Ezra. (2020). *Why We're Polarized*. New York: Simon & Schuster.

Levine, Peter A. (2010). *In an Unspoken Voice: How the Body Releases Trauma and Restores Goodness*. Berkeley, CA: North Atlantic Books.

Levitsky, Steven, and Daniel Ziblatt. (2018). *How Democracies Die*. New York: Crown Publishing.

Litwack, Leon F. (2009). *How Free Is Free? The Long Death of Jim Crow*. Cambridge, MA: Harvard University Press.

MacDonnell, Francis. (1994). "Reconstruction in the Wake of Vietnam: The Pardoning of Robert E. Lee and Jefferson Davis." *Civil War History* 40 (2), 119–133.

Morris, David J. (2015). *The Evil Hours: A Biography of Post-Traumatic Stress Disorder*. New York: Houghton Mifflin Harcourt.

Morrison, Toni. (1992). *Playing in the Dark: Whiteness and the Literary Imagination*. Cambridge, MA: Harvard University Press.

———. (2004). *Beloved*. New York: Vintage Books.

———. (2007). *Song of Solomon*. New York: Vintage Books.

Oklahoma Commission to Study the Tulsa Race Riot of 1921. (2001). In *Redress for Historical Injustices in the United States*, ed. Michael T. Martin and Marilyn Yaquinto, 642–644. Durham, NC: Duke University Press.

Opotow, Susan. (2005). "Hate, Conflict, and Moral Exclusion." In *The Psychology of Hate*, ed. Robert J. Sternberg, 121–153. Washington, D.C.: American Psychological Association.

———. (2008). "'Not So Much As Place to Lay Our Head . . .': Moral Inclusion and Exclusion in the American Civil War Reconstruction." *Social Justice Research* 1, 26–49.

Packard, Jerrold M. (2003). *American Nightmare: The History of Jim Crow*. New York: St. Martin's Press.

Rawls, John. (2009). *A Theory of Justice*. Cambridge, MA: Harvard University Press.

Reich, Wilhelm. (1970). *The Mass Psychology of Fascism*. New York: Macmillan.

Rothstein, Richard (2017). *The Color of Law: A Forgotten History of How Our Government Segregated America*. New York: Liveright Publishing.

Saul, Jack. (2013). *Collective Trauma, Collective Healing: Promoting Community Resilience in the Aftermath of Disaster*. New York: Routledge.

Scarry, Elaine. (1985). *The Body in Pain: The Making and Unmaking of the World*. New York: Oxford University Press.

Scharf, M. (2007). "Long-Term Effects of Trauma: Psychosocial Functioning of the Second and Third Generation of Holocaust Survivors." *Development and Psychopathology* 19 (2), 603–622.

Sexton, Jared Yates. (2020). *American Rule: How a Nation Conquered the World but Failed Its People*. New York: Dutton.

Sibrava, Nicholas J., et al. (2019). "Posttraumatic Stress Disorder in African American and Latinx Adults: Clinical Course and the Role of Racial and Ethnic Discrimination." *American Psychologist* 74 (1), 116.

Sigal, John J., and Vivian Rakoff. (1971). "Concentration Camp Survival: A Pilot Study of Effects on the Second Generation." *Canadian Psychiatric Association Journal* 5, 393–397.

Sinha, Manisha. (2003). *The Counterrevolution of Slavery: Politics and Ideology in Antebellum South Carolina*. Chapel Hill: University of North Carolina Press.

Smith, D. N. (2019). "Authoritarianism Reimagined: The Riddle of Trump's Base." *Sociological Quarterly* 2, 210–223.

Snyder, Timothy. (2017). *On Tyranny: Twenty Lessons from the Twentieth Century*. New York: Ten Speed Press.

Soboroff, Jacob. (2020). *Separated: Inside an American Tragedy*. New York: HarperCollins.

Solomon, Andrew. (2011). *The Noonday Demon: An Atlas of Depression*. New York: Simon & Schuster.

Stanley, Jason. (2018). *How Fascism Works: The Politics of Us and Them*. New York: Random House.

Stanton, William. (1960). *The Leopard's Spots: Scientific Attitudes Toward Race in America*. Chicago: University of Chicago Press.

Steele, Kathy, Suzette Boon, and Onno Hart. (2016). *Treating Trauma-Related Dissociation: A Practical, Integrative Approach*. New York: W. W. Norton.

Stenner, Karen. (2005). *The Authoritarian Dynamic*. Cambridge: Cambridge University Press.

———. (2009). "Three Kinds of 'Conservatism.'" *Psychological Inquiry* 2–3, 142–159.

———. (2020). "Authoritarianism: Liberal Democracy Has Now Exceeded Many People's Capacity to Tolerate It." *Hope Not Hate* 44.

Travis, Jeremy. (2005). *But They All Come Back: Facing the Challenges of Prisoner Reentry*. Washington, DC: Urban Institute Press.

van der Kolk, Bessel A. (2014). *The Body Keeps the Score: Brain, Mind, and Body in the Healing of Trauma*. New York: Viking Penguin.

van der Kolk, Bessel A., Alexander C. McFarlane, and Lars Weisaeth, editors. (2012). *Traumatic Stress*. New York: Guilford Press.

Walker, Pete. (2013). *Complex PTSD: From Surviving to Thriving: A Guide and Map for Recovering from Childhood Trauma*. CreateSpace Publishing.

Whitman, James Q. (2017). *Hitler's American Model: The United States and the Making of Nazi Race Law*. Princeton: Princeton University Press.

Wilkerson, Isabel. (2010). *The Warmth of Other Suns: The Epic Story of America's Great Migration*. New York: Vintage Books.

————. (2020). *Caste: The Origins of Our Discontents*. New York: Random House.

Wise, Tim J. (2008). *White Like Me: Reflections on Race from a Privileged Son*. New York: Counterpoint Press.

Wolynn, Mark. (2016). *It Didn't Start with You: How Inherited Family Trauma Shapes Who We Are and How to End the Cycle*. New York: Viking.

Woodward, Bob. (2020). *Rage*. New York: Simon & Schuster.

Yehuda, Rachel, and Amy Lehrner. (2018). "Intergenerational Transmission of Trauma Effects: Putative Role of Epigenetic Mechanisms." *World Psychiatry* 3, 243–257.

Yehuda, Rachel, Amy Lehrner, and Laura C. Pratchett. (2016). "Trauma- and Stressor-Related Disorders." In *Mount Sinai Expert Guides*, 103–112. Hoboken, NJ: John Wiley & Sons.

About the Author

Avary L. Trump

MARY L. TRUMP, Ph.D., is the author of the international #1 bestseller *Too Much and Never Enough: How My Family Created the World's Most Dangerous Man.* She holds a Ph.D. from the Derner Institute of Advanced Psychological Studies at Adelphi University and has taught graduate courses in trauma, psychopathology, and developmental psychology.